THE CHRONICLES OF
TRANSFORMATION

The Chronicles of Transformation

A Spiritual Journey with C. S. Lewis

Edited by
Leonard J. DeLorenzo

Illustrated by
Stephen Barany

IGNATIUS PRESS   SAN FRANCISCO

Cover art by Stephen Barany

Cover design by John Herreid

© 2022 by Ignatius Press, San Francisco
All rights reserved
ISBN 978-1-62164-535-1 (PB)
ISBN 978-1-64229-174-2 (eBook)
Library of Congress Control Number 2022930105
Printed in the United States of America ∞

CONTENTS

EDITOR'S PREFACE

In a world that becomes stale without wonder, how do you reimagine the drama and joy of Christianity? For C. S. Lewis, the answer was to invite us into a different world that would help us see this one with fresh eyes. That world was Narnia, and by writing that world into existence, Lewis created a land where courage would be tested and character forged, opening up the possibility for a moral and spiritual journey.

Lewis started writing the first of these chronicles because he had in his mind the image of a faun standing next to a lamppost, and he wanted to tell a story about what he saw. In the course of writing that first story, a golden lion suddenly appeared in his imagination, and before long, the entire narrative was being pulled toward the Lion, who would become this new world's redeemer, creator, and sanctifier. By his own testimony, Lewis did not set out to write Christian stories: the Christian elements came in on their own, like the Lion himself. The author's initial intention did not imprison his final purpose, so that by the time the last book in the series was published in 1956, Lewis had managed to create an adventure filled with beloved characters that did not tell children the truths of Christianity, but rather gave them images to show them true Christian beauty.[1]

---

[1] Regarding Lewis' intention in writing the chronicles, see C. S. Lewis, "Sometimes Fairy Stories May Say Best What's to Be Said," in *Of Other Worlds: Essays and Stories* (New York: Harcourt, 1994), 36. David Fagerberg deals with this in greater detail in the introduction to this volume.

There is something felicitously concordant between how Lewis' more limited intentions were reshaped for a larger purpose and how those who pass into Narnia within these stories are themselves reshaped. The children are stretched and challenged, tried and tested, prodded and pulled in ways they do not fully understand. Between the wardrobe in the first chronicle and the stable door in the last, they who began as ordinary and limited are slowly but boldly transformed. They become stronger, braver, tenderer, more filled with desire, more capacious and caring and charitable. That Lion who pushed his way into Lewis' stories changed everything and everyone. What began with a single image grew into chronicles of transformation.

What, then, do the children who read or listen to these chronicles find? Of course, they find the faun, just as they find centaurs, a dragon, a unicorn, and all manner of Talking Beasts. They find witches and dwarfs and monopods in a world of vast seas and underground realms and rolling hills and open deserts. Of course, they find the Lion that Lewis himself found. But without thinking about it or without even a hint of analyzation, children find more in these stories than what at first appears. They find themselves in the middle of betrayal and forgiveness; they are moved with others from cowardice to chivalry; they feel the cost of sacrifice and the danger of great deeds; they effortlessly and passionately care for a world that has become their own. And, without prompting, they begin to wait for and love that magnificent Lion.

Narnia is a place where the choices and actions, the desires and dispositions of children affect their own destinies and the fate of the world. It is a place where children learn what it means to grow in maturity, to become responsible, and to develop character. They learn what it means to love the one who calls them into being and who gives them a mission in life—a mission that matters on the grandest scale. Above all, what children learn in Narnia is the importance of remaining childlike. Narnia is a place where adults can always start over in relearning what is all too quickly forgotten.

The spiritual benefit of these stories is not intended for children alone. The benefit redounds to all who are childlike, as well as all those who will allow themselves to become so again. This includes adults who have been weighed down by life and those who have become too intellectually "puffed up" or too spiritually sophisticated to immerse themselves easily in chronicles like these.

For children and adults alike, the transformation does not happen aside from enjoying the chronicles, but happens precisely because they are enjoyed. That is the way to take these stories as seriously as possible: by enjoying them. The deeper purpose that Lewis found is opened to those who let themselves be pulled in. As the combined work of scholars and artists, this volume is an invitation to reopen the imagination and enjoy as adults what at first seem to be just stories for children.

The idea for this volume emerged from a series of popular lectures to accompany communal readings of the Chronicles of Narnia during the liturgical seasons of Lent and Easter. Reading the chronicles was not proposed as a substitute for prayer, fasting, and almsgiving, or as a substitute for reading Scripture. Instead, the hope in engaging these stories was to soften our defenses and open up space within our hearts and minds for welcoming the joy of Christ, in whom the drama of all life bursts forth. This is especially important for those worn down by the trials of life.

In one of his own literary essays, Lewis wrote that we must "surrender ourselves with childlike attention to the mood of the story" if we are to enjoy it.[2] To study the story—to "contemplate" it, as he puts the matter in *Surprised by Joy*—is not the same as enjoying. To enjoy, you must be "in it" in such a way that your whole imagination is engaged, whereas reflecting on the story takes you at least one step away from that total surrender.[3]

Elsewhere, Lewis provided an anecdote to help explain the difference. He tells of standing in a pitch-black toolshed where the only source of light came through a small hole in the ceiling. Standing in the corner of the shed, he could look at the light, think about the light, maybe even marvel at the light. But moving right beneath that hole in the ceiling and thus standing *in* the beam of light changed everything. Along that beam, he looked up to see the trees and leaves and the expansive world outside; he could see the sky and glimpse the radiance of the sun some ninety-three million miles away. The first experience is looking *at* the light; the second is looking *along* the light.[4] What Lewis means by "contemplation" is aligned with the first kind of looking, and "enjoyment" with the second. Perhaps the greatest benefit of contemplation in this sense, then, is to help you recognize the difference light makes and to know something about the light you learn to see by. It is good to know about light; it is better to live in the light.

[2] C. S. Lewis, "Edmund Spenser, 1552–1599," in *Studies in Medieval and Renaissance Literature*, ed. Walter Hooper (Cambridge: Cambridge University Press, 1966), 137, quoted in Michael Ward, *Planet Narnia: The Seven Heavens in the Imagination of C. S. Lewis* (New York: Oxford University Press, 2008), 18.

[3] The way in which Lewis distinguishes between "Contemplation" and "Enjoyment" when speaking of his own conversion (or "re-version") is instructive here. See C. S. Lewis, *Surprised by Joy* (New York: Harcourt Brace, 1955), 217–19.

[4] C. S. Lewis, "Meditation in a Toolshed," in *God in the Dock* (New York: Inspirational, 1996), 442–44.

What you will find in this volume will help you contemplate Lewis' masterpiece. That means you will be prompted to reflect, to reconsider, and to begin to wonder at what the Chronicles of Narnia give us to enjoy. Indeed, our aim is to prepare you to enjoy the chronicles on a return visit—especially as an adult—while also guiding you to deepen your appreciation of what you may have previously already enjoyed. We look at the light with you, though each of us who contributed to this work has also stood in the light and enjoyed the warmth of the Narnian sun.

In the introductory chapter "Arriving at Narnia," David Fagerberg prepares us to enter by teaching us to expect not allegory but what Lewis calls "supposal." We are nudged away from tidy point-by-point connections between Narnia and our world, and encouraged toward the kind of imaginative freedom that allows Narnia's enchantments to disenchant us from worldliness. The seven subsequent chapters guide us through the seven chronicles, one at a time. I take us through *The Lion, the Witch and the Wardrobe* to notice the hidden workings of sacrificial love and the deep places in which that love moves. Father Michael Ward takes us into the atmosphere of *Prince Caspian* where we are acquainted with and indeed delighted by what it feels like to live inside a chivalric tradition. Peter Schakel breaks open *The Voyage of the "Dawn Treader"* to trace the new directions Lewis explores therein as he moves us further and further away from settled complacency and toward the horizon of myth. Rebekah Lamb reveals how much Lewis cares for the kind of person one becomes and how *The Silver Chair* is, in large part, an immersion into a certain kind of education. Francesca Aran Murphy stirs up the longing for home and true freedom in *The Horse and His Boy*, which, as she shows with repeated appeals to *Surprised by Joy*, is the most autobiographical of Lewis' seven chronicles. Catherine Rose Cavadini follows the creation of Narnia in *The Magician's Nephew* and illuminates the biblical calling to "dominion" proper to those who are to live in harmony with him who sang this world into existence. And finally, Anthony Pagliarini takes us to the beginning of the end of all things in Narnia, when sin and judgment, deception and fidelity, death and endless life all hang in the balance in *The Last Battle*.

At the portal to each of the chapters, we are treated to original works of art that deepen and stretch our rediscovery of Narnia in distinct and delightful ways. Madeline Infantine's poem sequence, "On Knowing Him Here for a Little," draws from the inconsolable longing for the subtle and supreme power of that golden Lion who lives within and behind all stories. Stephen Barany's series of illustrations opens up a symphonic dialogue between the chronicles themselves, the poems that muse on them, and the prose that contemplates them.

The order in which we read and reflect on the chronicles in this volume is, as you likely already noticed, the order in which they were published, rather than the chronological order within the narratives themselves. Our ordering of the chronicles is at odds with the volume that I have used throughout to cite references from the books, which (foolishly, in our view) presents the chronicles in the other order. Both Peter Schakel and I comment on this in our essays, and Michael Ward has addressed this issue in other writings,[5] but here at the outset we "defend" this decision (sometimes people work up strong opinions about it) by

---

[5] See Michael Ward, "Does This Discovery Affect the Order in Which the Books Should Be Read?," *Michael Ward* (blog), last accessed August 11, 2021, http://michaelward.net/faqs/.

saying that putting *The Lion, the Witch and the Wardrobe* first preserves the order of discovery. We pass into Narnia for the first time with Lucy. Her wonder becomes ours. That would be reason enough for holding to this order; plus, nothing at all is lost if *The Magician's Nephew* is sixth rather than first. In fact, the creation account seems quite at home right before the story of the end. Beginnings and endings go together nicely.

Though this volume is not the thing itself that is to be "enjoyed," on behalf of my fellow contributors I do say that I hope you enjoy this volume. Even more, I hope that it leads you to greater enjoyment, first in the Chronicles of Narnia and then, ultimately, in that wider, grander, lovelier place to which we are all being drawn.

Leonard J. DeLorenzo
South Bend, Indiana

INTRODUCTION

Arriving at Narnia

David W. Fagerberg

The first of the Chronicles of Narnia was published in 1950, followed by six others. Over the decades since, parents have read these books to their children as bedtime stories, and children have read them for themselves when they got a little older. That is probably the most profitable way to explore Narnia. But can grown-ups return to Narnia, as this collection of essays asks grown-ups to do? Lewis left three pieces of advice for them as they make this attempt.

The first piece of advice concerns the person of Susan, when it is revealed that she does not return to Narnia in *The Last Battle*:

> "Oh Susan!" said Jill. "She's interested in nothing nowadays except nylons and lipstick and invitations. She always was a jolly site too keen on being grown-up."
>
> "Grown-up, indeed," said the Lady Polly. "I wish she would grow up. She wasted all her school time, wanting to be the age she is now, and shall waste all the rest of her life trying to stay that age. Her whole idea is to race on to the silliest time of one's life as quick as she can and then stop there as long as she can."[1]

Hers is a mistake we hope we do not make.

[1] C. S. Lewis, *The Last Battle*, in *The Chronicles of Narnia* (New York: Harper-Collins, 2001), 741, chap. 12. Throughout *The Chronicles of Transformation*, all

The second piece of advice comes from the person of Lucy, who learns a fact upon her return to Narnia in *Prince Caspian*:

"Welcome, child," [Aslan] said.
  "Aslan," said Lucy, "you're bigger."
  "That is because you are older, little one," answered he.
  "Not because you are?"
  "I am not. But every year you grow, you will find me bigger."[2]

The third and final piece of advice comes from Lewis directly, in his dedication of *The Lion, the Witch and the Wardrobe*. It goes to Lucy Barfield, daughter of his good friend Owen Barfield.

My Dear Lucy,
  I wrote this story for you, but when I began it I had not realized that girls grow quicker than books. As a result you are already too old for fairy tales, and by the time it is printed and bound you will be older still. But some day you will be old enough to start reading fairy tales again. You can then take it down from some upper shelf, dust it, and tell me what you think of it. I shall probably be too deaf to hear, and too old to understand, a word you say, but I shall still be

your affectionate Godfather,
C. S. Lewis[3]

---

citations to the books in the Narnia series—*The Lion, the Witch and the Wardrobe, Prince Caspian, The Voyage of the "Dawn Treader," The Silver Chair, The Horse and His Boy, The Magician's Nephew, The Last Battle*—come from the 2001 single-volume edition by HarperCollins.
  [2] *Prince Caspian*, 380, chap. 10.
  [3] *The Lion, the Witch and the Wardrobe*, 110.

Both the grown-up authors and the grown-up readers of these essays hope that they are not too old for fairy tales, that they can find Aslan bigger upon this return to them, and that they will be rewarded in their search for the theological treasures Lewis has hidden in the stories.

That search will be conducted within each chronicle, by the author to whom it is assigned. My task here is simply to give some background to the writing of the stories. What motivated Lewis? How does he mean for us to read his stories?

A Different Kind of Story

Are the chronicles extended allegories? Lewis emphatically denies it: "Some people seem to think that I began by asking myself how I could say something about Christianity to children; then fixed on the fairy tale as an instrument; then collected information about child-psychology and decided what age group I'd write for; then drew up a list of basic Christian truths and hammered out 'allegories' to embody them. This is all pure moonshine."[4]

Lewis knew allegory. He knew how to read it and how to write it. An example of the former comes from his day job as an Oxford don. In the study that would establish his academic reputation, *The Allegory of Love*, he analyzes almost two dozen medieval allegorical authors and concludes that "allegory, in some sense, belongs not to medieval man but to man, or even to mind, in general. It is of the very nature of thought and language to represent what is immaterial in picturable terms," which is why "you can

[4] C. S. Lewis, "Sometimes Fairy Stories May Say Best What's to Be Said," in *Of Other Worlds: Essays and Stories* (New York: Harcourt, 1994), 36.

start with an immaterial fact, such as the passions which you actually experience, and can then invent *visibilia* to express them."[5] An example of the latter comes from the first book he wrote after his conversion. It is titled *The Pilgrim's Regress*, but its subtitle further reveals that he offers it as *An Allegorical Apology for Christianity, Reason, and Romanticism*. There we meet such allegorical figures as Lady Reason, Mother Kirk, and Father History. But this is not how the chronicles came about, and thinking so is pure moonshine. We can finish the quote: "I couldn't write in that way at all. Everything began with images: a faun carrying an umbrella, a queen on a sledge, a magnificent lion. At first there wasn't even anything Christian about them; that element pushed itself in of its own accord. It was part of the bubbling."[6]

So if the chronicles are not allegories, what are they? Lewis can offer us just the word for them. He mentions it in this concise reply to an adult inquirer: "The Narnian books are not as much allegory as supposal. 'Suppose there were a Narnian world and it, like ours, needed redemption. What kind of incarnation and Passion might Christ be supposed to undergo *there*?'"[7]

Lewis fleshes out this idea of "supposal literature" in a number of replies to another set of correspondents. Lewis tried to answer every letter he received, including letters he received from children. His replies have been gathered in a

---

[5] C. S. Lewis, *The Allegory of Love* (London: Oxford University Press, 1951), 44–45. It is interesting to note that Lewis dedicated this book to Lucy's father, Owen Barfield: "To Owen Barfield, wisest and best of my unofficial teachers." Barfield, in turn, dedicated his most famous book, *Poetic Diction*, to Lewis. "To C. S. Lewis. 'Opposition is true friendship.'" One can sense the pleasure they both derived from their intellectual jousts.

[6] Lewis, "Sometimes Fairy Stories May Say Best What's to Be Said," 36.

[7] James E. Higgins, "A Letter from C. S. Lewis," *Horn Book*, October 19, 1966, https://www.hbook.com/story/a-letter-from-c-s-lewis.

book titled *Letters to Children*, and although we have only Lewis' letters, not the children's (leaving us in the position of listening in on one end of a phone conversation), we can deduce what the children asked from the answers that Lewis gives them. He reveals what he intended in several of the letters:

> Dear Fifth Graders
>
> I am so glad you liked the Narnian books and it was very kind of you to write and tell me....
>
> You are mistaken when you think that everything in the books "represents" something in this world. Things do that in *The Pilgrim's Progress* but I'm not writing in that way. I did not say to myself "Let us represent Jesus as He really is in our world by a Lion in Narnia": I said "Let us *suppose* that there were a land like Narnia and that the Son of God, as He became a Man in our world, became a Lion there, and then imagine what would happen." If you think about it, you will see that it is quite a different thing.[8]

Lewis writes something very similar in a reply he makes to a young lady named Patricia, who was thirteen at the time: "*All* your points are in a sense, right. But I'm not exactly 'representing' the real (Christian) story in symbols. I'm more saying 'Suppose there were a world like Narnia and it needed rescuing and the Son of God (or the "Great Emperor oversea") went to redeem *it*, as He

---

[8] C.S. Lewis, *Letters to Children* (New York: Macmillan, 1985), 45. Lewis' kindness and geniality is revealed in many of these letters. For example, this one ends with him writing, "I'm tall, fat, rather bald, red-faced, double-chinned, black-haired, have a deep voice, and wear glasses for reading. The only way for us to Aslan's country is through death, as far as I know: perhaps some very good people get just a tiny glimpse before then. Best love to you all. When you say your prayers sometimes ask God to bless me."

came to redeem ours, what might it, in that world, all have been like?' Perhaps it comes to much the same thing as you thought, but not quite."[9] And one can imagine what was in the letter from a young lady named Phyllida when Lewis replies, "I'm not quite sure what you mean about 'silly adventure stories without any point.' If they *are* silly, then having a point won't save them."[10] He goes on to disagree that there is some "point" that is a truth about the real world which one can take *out of* the story. Indeed, "I think that *looking for* a 'point' in that sense may prevent one sometimes from getting the real effect of the story in itself."[11] But he ends by complimenting her on a remark she has made, and enlarging it: "P.S. Of course you're right about the Narnian books being better than the tracts; at least, in the way a picture is better than a map."[12] He is referring to the series of ninety tracts produced in the nineteenth-century Oxford movement to explain Christian doctrine. Narnia is better than the tracts the way a picture is better than a map.

Can we think of the reasons why we might prefer to have a picture of the Alps instead of a book that gives us the longitude and latitude? Might the picture create a stronger feeling in us? It would fall short to describe the purpose of the chronicles as nothing more than wanting to create a "feeling," but they do create an exclamation in us. Of course! This would be Christ's reaction if he came across the situation. Of course! Christ would instruct his kings and queens in Narnia this way. Of course! Sin works like this, and redemption has this cost, and Aslan wants to develop these virtues in us.

[9] Ibid., 93.
[10] Ibid., 35.
[11] Ibid.
[12] Ibid., 36.

connection between Lewis' supposal literature and real
life that would please him very much. This one is written
to an adult: the mother of a nine-year-old boy. It is easy
to deduce the concern the mother expressed in her letter
from Lewis' first paragraph:

> Dear Mrs. K ... ,
>   Tell Laurence from me, with my love:
>   1/ Even if he was loving Aslan more than Jesus (I'll
> explain in a moment why he can't really be doing this)
> he would not be an idol-worshipper. If he was an idol-
> worshipper he'd be doing it on purpose, whereas he's now
> doing it because he can't help doing it, and trying hard not
> to do it....
>   2/ But Laurence can't *really* love Aslan more than Jesus,
> even if he feels that's what he is doing. For the things he
> loves Aslan for doing or saying are simply the things Jesus
> really did and said. So that when Laurence thinks he is
> loving Aslan, he is really loving Jesus: and perhaps loving
> Him more than he ever did before.[13]

Lewis admits that Aslan has one thing Jesus does not—the
body of a lion—but adds that if Christ were to save other
worlds he might have taken all sorts of bodies, and God
knows that a little boy's imagination will find talking and
friendly animals very attractive; therefore Lewis does not
think God minds if Laurence likes the lion body.

Supposal literature doesn't represent, doesn't substitute
for, doesn't allegorize. It touches, it awakens, it shows
something—which is how Paul Holmer describes not only
the chronicles, but the whole idea of "mere Christianity"
as presented across Lewis' entire corpus:

[13] Ibid., 52.

In brief, then, Lewis's literature shows us something without quite arguing it.... Lewis would have it that literature actually creates thoughts in us; it is not only about thoughts, it causes them to exist. It is as if literature is not a description of emotions; rather, it so describes states of affairs that the ordinate emotions are invested in us. Literature is not about existence so much as it is an addition to it. It gives us experiences, feelings, moral pangs, wishes, hopes that we have never had.... [Literature] communicates in such a way that, when successful, it creates new capabilities and capacities, powers and a kind of roominess in the human personality. One becomes susceptible to new competencies, new functions, new pathos and possibilities.[14]

I think this idea of literature "showing us something" is an appropriate way to describe what both Lewis and J. R. R. Tolkien came to believe about fairytales and mythology, and it was a topic they appear to have discussed during the decade of 1930 (likely over more than one pint of beer at the Eagle and Child).

Lewis, Tolkien, and the Power of Myth

The story of Lewis' conversion after a stroll down Addison's Walk with Tolkien and Victor Dyson on a September night in 1931 is well known. Lewis never underestimated the power of myth. In his autobiography, he admits that "I came far nearer to feeling [worship and awe] about the

---

[14] Paul L. Holmer, *C. S. Lewis: The Shape of His Faith and Thought* (New York: Harper and Row, 1976), 20. In the preface, Holmer tells the story of having sent an angry and impetuous letter to Lewis, and having received a reply "so full of charity and plain wisdom that it made at least this then frustrated and distraught student see very clearly how tangled his own life actually was" (p. ix).

Norse gods whom I disbelieved in than I had ever done about the true God while I believed."[15] Nevertheless, Lewis had argued during that late-night walk that myths are "lies breathed through silver," and his two companions were trying to disabuse him of that mistake. Humphrey Carpenter has reconstructed the conversation by consolidating other sources (letters, later accounts):

> No, said Tolkien, they are not lies.... You look at trees, he said, and call them "trees," and probably you do not think twice about the word. You call a star a "star," and think nothing more of it. But you must remember that these words, "tree," "star," were (in their original forms) names given to these objects by people with very different views from yours. To you, a tree is simply a vegetable organism, and a star simply a ball of inanimate matter moving along a mathematical course. But the first men to talk of "trees" and "stars" saw things very differently. To them the world was alive with mythological beings.[16]

Humphrey summarizes Tolkien's point in his own words: "In practicing 'mythopoeia' and peopling the world with elves and dragons and goblins, a story-teller, or 'sub-creator' as Tolkien liked to call such a person, is actually fulfilling God's purpose, and reflecting a splintered fragment of the true light. Pagan myths are therefore never just 'lies': there is always something of the truth in them."[17]

So myth might have an inkling (pun intended) of truth, but Lewis still could not grasp how the life and death of someone two thousand years ago could help us here and now. He had ridiculed concepts like propitiation, sacrifice,

---

[15] C. S. Lewis, *Surprised by Joy* (New York: Harcourt Brace, 1955), 77.

[16] Humphrey Carpenter, *The Inklings: C. S. Lewis, J. R. R. Tolkien, Charles Williams, and Their Friends* (New York: Ballantine Books, 1978), 146–48.

[17] Ibid., 46–47.

and blood of the lamb in his agnostic years. How could Christ's death save the world? And to this Tolkien had an immediate answer.

> Had he not shown how pagan myths were, in fact, God expressing himself through the minds of poets, and using the images of their "mythopoeia" to express fragments of his eternal truth? Well then, Christianity (he said) is exactly the same thing—with the enormous difference that the poet who invented it was God Himself, and the images He used were real men and actual history.
>
> Do you mean, asked Lewis, that the death and resurrection of Christ is the old "dying god" story all over again?
>
> Yes, Tolkien answered, except that here is a *real* Dying God, with a precise location in history and definite historical consequences. The old myth has become a fact. But it still retains the character of a myth.[18]

Lewis got the point: the gospel is a "true myth." This especially resonated with him in conjunction with G. K. Chesterton's *The Everlasting Man*. He writes in his autobiography, "The question was no longer to find the one simply true religion among a thousand religions simply false. It was rather, 'Where has religion reached its true maturity? Where, if anywhere, have the hints of all Paganism been fulfilled?... Where was the thing full grown?'... (*The Everlasting Man* was helping me here.)"[19] Twelve days later Lewis wrote to his friend Arthur Greeves that the idea of Christianity being a "true myth" was working on his mind:

> Now what Dyson and Tolkien showed me was this: that if I met the idea of sacrifice in a Pagan story I didn't mind it at all: again, that if I met the idea of god sacrificing himself

[18] Ibid., 47–48.
[19] Lewis, *Surprised by Joy*, 235.

to himself ... I liked it very much ... provided I met it anywhere *except* in the Gospels....

Now the story of Christ is simply a true myth: a myth working on us in the same way as the others, but with this tremendous difference that *it really happened*.... Does this amount to a belief in Christianity? At any rate I am now certain (a) that this Christian story is to be approached, in a sense, as I approach the other myths; (b) that it is the most important and full of meaning. I am also *nearly* certain that it really happened.[20]

Tolkien continued thinking about the subject by writing a poem that reflects the conversation, which has come to be called "Mythopoeia" (he says he wrote it while "invigilating exams"—proctoring students in their exam room—which seems a good use of time). According to his son Christopher, there are seven extant versions of the poem[21] and Tolkien made the intended recipient increasingly clear. On a fifth version, Tolkien wrote "JRRT for CSL," and on the sixth he added "Philomythus Misomytho"—from the myth lover (Tolkien) to the myth hater (Lewis). We will here quote only the opening lines:

> You look at trees and label them just so,
> (for trees are "trees", and growing is "to grow");
> you walk the earth and tread with solemn pace
> one of the many minor globes of Space:
> a star's a star, some matter in a ball
> compelled to courses mathematical
> amid the regimented, cold, inane,
> where destined atoms are each moment slain.[22]

---

[20] C. S. Lewis, *They Stand Together: The Letters of C. S. Lewis to Arthur Greeves,* ed. Walter Hooper (London: Collins, 1979), 431.

[21] Christopher Tolkien, preface to *Tree and Leaf,* by J. R. R. Tolkien (London: HarperCollins, 2001), vii.

[22] J. R. R. Tolkien, "Mythopoeia," in *Tree and Leaf,* 85.

The difference between what science sees and what myth sees is handily expressed by Lewis in *The Voyage of the "Dawn Treader"* when the children meet Ramandu. He is a star retired from the celestial dance, but to whom every morning a bird brings a fire-berry to make him young again, until he can once more tread the great dance. To this, the visitor from our world named Eustace says, "In our world ... a star is a huge ball of flaming gas." Ramandu corrects him, saying, "Even in your world, my son, that is not what a star is but only what it is made of."[23]

Tolkien and Lewis had been talking about what is real and what is really real, what something is made of and what it really is, and how to show the reality beneath the surface. Those glimpses are what they both loved in the old literature, as Tolkien remembers in one of his letters. "As C.S. Lewis said to me long ago, more or less—(I do not suppose my memory of his *dicta* is any more precisely accurate than his of mine: I often find strange things attributed to me in his works)—'if they won't write the kind of books we want to read, we shall have to write them ourselves; but it is very laborious.'"[24] And so they did. They initially thought this goal could be served by science fiction, and they struck a bargain that Lewis would write on space travel and Tolkien on time travel. Tolkien's work was never completed; Lewis' appeared as the Space Trilogy. But the further Tolkien got into the land of the Hobbit, the more he thought of the nature of Faerie, and in 1939 (eight years after the discussion on Addison's Walk), he delivered the Andrew Lang lecture at the University of St. Andrews, Scotland. We will return

---

[23] C.S. Lewis, *The Voyage of the "Dawn Treader,"* 522, chap. 14.

[24] *The Letters of J.R.R. Tolkien*, ed. Humphrey Carpenter (Boston: Houghton Mifflin Company, 1981), 209.

soon to what Lewis has to say about fairy stories, but it is interesting to glance at Tolkien's lecture while holding the Chronicles of Narnia in mind.

Tolkien argues that "a 'fairy-story' is one which touches on or uses Faerie, whatever its own main purpose may be: satire, adventure, morality, fantasy. Faerie itself may perhaps most nearly be translated by Magic—but it is magic of a peculiar mood and power, at the furthest pole from the vulgar devices of the laborious, scientific, magician."[25] Such fairy stories are not necessarily—i.e., not by necessity—intended for children:

> The common opinion seems to be that there is a natural connection between the minds of children and fairy-stories, of the same order as the connection between children's bodies and milk. I think this is an error; at best an error of false sentiment, and one that is therefore most often made by those who tend to think of children as a special kind of creature, almost a different race, rather than as normal, if immature, members of a particular family, and of the human family at large.[26]

Faerie is an atmosphere, a coloring, and begins with man as a subcreator. In Tolkien's experience, the enjoyment of the story was *not* dependent on the belief that such things could happen in real life. At the heart of the desire of Faerie is "the making or glimpsing of Other-worlds."[27]

In his conclusion, Tolkien identifies four values and functions of fairy stories. The first is *fantasy*, whereby "the human mind is capable of forming mental images of things not actually present. The faculty of conceiving the images

[25] J. R. R. Tolkien, "On Fairy-Stories," in *Tree and Leaf*, 10.
[26] Ibid., 34.
[27] Ibid., 41.

is called imagination."[28] To make images of things not in
the primary world is a virtue, not a vice. The second is
recovery, which is the regaining of a clear view: "We need
to clean our windows; so that the things seen clearly may
be freed from the drab blur of triteness or familiarity."[29]
Humility could also perform this service, if only we pos-
sessed it. The third is *escape*, used with a nonpejorative
tone. It is practical, even heroic, under the right circumstances: "Why should a man be scorned, if, finding himself
in prison, he tries to get out and go home? ... The critics
have chosen the wrong word, and, what is more, they are
confusing the Escape of the Prisoner with the Flight of
the Deserter."[30] Fairy stories have more permanent things
to talk about than electric lamps—lightning, for example.
Therefore, "we should not be ashamed of the 'escape' of
archaism: of preferring not dragons but horses, castles, sail-
ing ships, bows and arrows; not only elves, but knights and
kings and priests."[31] And the fourth is *consolation*, although
that word does not quite express it. Tolkien will have
to create one: "Tragedy is the true form of Drama ...,
but the opposite is true of Fairy-story. Since we do not
appear to possess a word that expresses this opposite—I
will call it Eucatastrophe."[32] It is the consolation of the
happy ending, and all fairy stories must have it in order
to be complete. It consists of "the good catastrophe, the
sudden joyous turn: this joy, which is one of the things
which fairy tales can produce supremely well, is not essentially 'escapist' nor 'fugitive'. In its fairytale setting, it is a
sudden and miraculous grace: never to be counted on to

[28] Ibid., 46.
[29] Ibid., 48.
[30] Ibid., 60–61.
[31] Ibid., 63.
[32] Ibid., 68.

return."[33] It catches our breath and lifts the heart when the "turn" comes. Tolkien provides additional description of eucatastrophe in one of his letters:

> And I concluded by saying that the Resurrection was the greatest "eucatastrophe" possible in the greatest Fairy Story—and produces that essential emotion: Christian joy which produces tears because it is qualitatively so like sorrow, because it comes from those places where Joy and Sorrow are one, reconciled, as selfishness and altruism are lost in Love. Of course I do not mean that the Gospels tell what is *only* a fairy-story; but I do mean very strongly that they do tell a fairy-story: the greatest. Man the story-teller would have to be redeemed in a manner consonant with his nature: by a moving story.... To descend to lesser things: I knew I had written the story of worth in *The Hobbit* when reading it (after it was old enough to be detached from me) I had suddenly in a fairly strong measure the eucatastrophic emotion at Bilbo's exclamation: "the Eagles! The Eagles are coming!"[34]

Lewis also reflects upon the value of stories, storytelling, and fairy stories, and we can see overlaps with Tolkien on numerous points. For example, both agree that "a children's story which is enjoyed only by children is a bad children's story."[35] Neither Lewis nor Tolkien denigrate imagination: "For me, reason is the natural organ of truth; but imagination is the organ of meaning. Imagination, producing new metaphors or revivifying old, is not the cause of truth, but its condition."[36] Furthermore, both of

[33] Ibid., 68–69.

[34] *Letters of Tolkien*, 100.

[35] C. S. Lewis, "On Three Ways of Writing for Children," in *Of Other Worlds*, 24.

[36] C. S. Lewis, *Selected Literary Essays*, ed. Walter Hooper (Cambridge: Cambridge University Press, 1969), 265.

them find the storyteller to be a subcreator: "The appeal
of the fairy story lies in the fact that man there most fully
exercises his function as a 'subcreator.'"[37] Lewis says he
was exercising his prerogative of being subcreator—i.e.,
the prerogative of a human being—when he began seeing
pictures in his head.

> The Editor has asked me to tell you how I came to write
> *The Lion, the Witch and the Wardrobe*. I will try, but you
> must not believe all the authors tell you about how they
> wrote their books. This is not because they mean to tell
> lies. It is because a man writing a story is too excited about
> the story itself to sit back and notice how he is doing it.
> In fact, that might stop the works; just as, if you started
> thinking about how you tie your tie, the next thing is that
> you find you can't tie it. And afterwards, when the story
> is finished, he has forgotten a good deal of what writing
> it was like.
>
> One thing I am sure of. All my seven Narnian books,
> and my three science fiction books, began with seeing pic-
> tures in my head. At first they were not a story, just pic-
> tures. The *Lion* all began with a picture of a Faun carrying
> an umbrella and parcels in the snowy wood. This picture
> had been in my mind since I was about sixteen. Then one
> day, when I was about forty, I said to myself: "Let's try to
> make a story about it."[38]

Both Lewis and Tolkien attribute to the story itself
some mysterious power that eludes control of the author.
Concerning his lack of control over certain developments
in *The Lord of the Rings*, Tolkien confesses in one letter that
"a new character has come on the scene (I'm sure I did not

---

[37] Lewis, "On Three Ways of Writing for Children," 27.
[38] C. S. Lewis, "It All Began with a Picture," in *Of Other Worlds*, 42.

invent him, I did not even want him, though I like him
...)."[39] And in another letter: "I met a lot of things on the
way that astonished me. Tom Bombadil I knew already;
but I had never been to Bree. Strider sitting in the corner
in the inn was a shock, and I had no more idea who he was
than had Frodo."[40]

Concerning his own lack of control, Lewis writes: "At
first I had very little idea how the story would go. But
then suddenly Aslan came bounding into it. I think I had
been having a good many dreams of lions about that time.
Apart from that, I don't know where the Lion came from
or why He came. But once He was there He pulled the
whole story together, and soon He pulled the other six
Narnian stories in after Him."[41]

Picture preceded form, and Lewis confesses not to
know exactly where the pictures came from. "I have never
exactly 'made' a story. With me the process is much more
like bird-watching than like either talking or building. I see
pictures. Some of these pictures have a common flavour,
almost a common smell, which groups them together."[42]
Then that picture went in search of a form. It found the
fairy tale: "And the moment I thought of that I fell in love
with the Form itself: its brevity, its severe restraints on
description, its flexible traditionalism, its inflexible hostility
to all analysis, digression, reflections and 'gas'. I was now
enamored of it. Its very limitations of vocabulary became
an attraction; as the hardness of the stone pleases the sculp-
tor or the difficulty of the sonnet delights the sonneteer."[43]
I daresay that this description of why the author loved the

---

[39] *Letters of Tolkien*, 79.

[40] Ibid., 216.

[41] Lewis, "It All Began with a Picture," 42.

[42] Lewis, "On Three Ways of Writing for Children," 32.

[43] Lewis, "Sometimes Fairy Stories May Say Best What's to Be Said," 36–37.

form of the fairy tale is also a description of why readers love the form of the chronicles: flexible traditionalism and hostility to analysis, along with limitations on vocabulary. Lewis has a character in *Out of the Silent Planet* express the same thought: " 'The best poetry, then, comes in the roughest speech?' 'Perhaps,' said the pfifltrigg. 'As the best pictures are made in the hardest stone.' "[44]

One of the values of casting his picture in the hard stone of fairy tale is that children know the best stories must be read repeatedly in order to be absorbed. "We do not enjoy a story fully at the first reading. Not till the curiosity, the sheer narrative lust, has been given its sop and laid asleep, are we at leisure to savor the real beauties. Till then, it is like wasting a great wine on a ravenous natural thirst which merely wants cold wetness. The children understand this well when they ask for the same story over and over again, and in the same words."[45] The children have higher interests than the plot. To Lewis, the plot "is really only a net whereby to catch something else. The real theme may be, and perhaps usually is, something that has no sequence in it, something other than a process and much more like a state or quality."[46]

First came the picture, and Lewis wanted to carve it in the hardest stone; then came the form into which he would do so; and only at the end, Lewis says, did he discover another motive within himself:

Then of course the Man in me began to have its turn. I thought I saw how stories of this kind could steal past a certain inhibition which had paralysed much of my own religion in childhood. Why did one find it so hard to feel

[44] C. S. Lewis, *Out of the Silent Planet* (New York: Scribner, 2003), 114.
[45] C. S. Lewis, "On Stories," in *Of Other Worlds*, 18.
[46] Ibid.

as one was told one ought to feel about God or about the sufferings of Christ? I thought the chief reason was that one was told one ought to. An obligation to feel can freeze feelings. And reverence itself did harm. The whole subject was associated with lowered voices; almost as if it were something medical. But supposing that by casting all these things into an imaginary world, stripping them of their stained-glass and Sunday school associations, one could make them for the first time appear in their real potency? Could one not thus steal past those watchful dragons? I thought one could.[47]

The Chronicles of Narnia serve many purposes.

Romance beyond Criticism

There are people who dislike fairy tales, Lewis is sad to admit. They have their various reasons. First, some people think fairy tales are too scary for children. Lewis replies that if you only read stories "in which nothing at all alarming ever happens, you would fail to banish the terrors, and would succeed in banishing all that can ennoble them or make them endurable." "Since it is so likely that they will meet cruel enemies, let them at least have heard of brave knights and heroic courage."[48] Second, some people think fairy tales will cause children to confuse fact with fancy. Lewis replies, "Does anyone suppose that [the child] really and prosaically longs for all the dangers and discomforts of the fairy tale?—really wants dragons in contemporary England?"[49] Third, some people think fairy tales

---

[47] Lewis, "Sometimes Fairy Stories May Say Best What's to Be Said," 37.
[48] Lewis, "On Three Ways of Writing for Children," 31–32.
[49] Ibid., 29.

are childish and we should outgrow them. Lewis replies: "A children's story which is enjoyed only by children is a bad children's story.... No book is really worth reading at the age of ten which is not equally worth reading at the age of fifty—except, of course, books of information."[50] And fourth, some people think fairy tales will make the real world seem dull. Lewis replies: "Paradoxically enough, it strengthens our relish for real life. This excursion into the preposterous sends us back with renewed pleasure to the actual.... [The child] does not despise real woods because he has read of enchanted woods: the reading makes all real woods a little enchanted."[51] Far from dulling the world, the excursion into fairyland gives the world a new dimension of depth. "It would be much truer to say that fairy land arouses [in the child] a longing for he knows not what."[52]

Lewis says, "I am not quite sure what made me, in a particular year of my life, feel that not only a fairy tale, but a fairy tale addressed to children, was exactly what I must write—or burst,"[53] but I think we have a hint of an answer in his last point above. Fairyland arouses a longing for . . . we know not what, he says. This is Lewis' notion of romance. The Chronicles of Narnia may be called romantic literature if, and only if, we enlarge our ordinary understanding of the term. Twice.

Our common understanding of romance is an emotional attachment between two people, but Lewis expands the

[50] Lewis, "On Stories," 15. One is reminded of Eustace Scrubb who "liked books if they were books of information and had pictures of grain elevators or of fat foreign children doing exercises in model schools" and didn't know what to expect to find in a dragon's lair because he "had read only the wrong books. They had a lot to say about exports and imports and governments and drains, but they were weak on dragons" (The Voyage of the "Dawn Treader," 425, chap. 1).

[51] Lewis, "On Three Ways of Writing for Children," 29–30.

[52] Ibid.

[53] Ibid., 28.

word a first time to a range of meanings it has in literary usage, ultimately identifying seven such usages. He names dangerous adventure; the marvelous, high-flown sentiments and titanic characters; indulgence in abnormal and antinatural moods; egoism and subjectivism; revolt against civilized conventions; and a sensibility to natural objects become solemn and enthusiastic. Then Lewis expands the word "romance" a second time when he states that "what I meant by Romanticism when I wrote *The Pilgrim's Regress* ... was not exactly any one of these seven."[54] Instead, he is trying to get at a certain deep experience, one he remembers from early childhood: "What I meant was a particular recurrent experience which dominated my childhood and adolescence and which I hastily called Romantic because inanimate nature and marvellous literature were among the things that evoked it."[55] In his autobiography, he mentions three such experiences: the memory of a morning house in the hills, the story of squirrel Nutkin that conveyed the idea of autumn, and the poetry of Longfellow. The quality common to these three experiences is that they each caused the experience of "an unsatisfied desire which is itself more desirable than any other satisfaction. I call it Joy, which is here a technical term and must be sharply distinguished both from Happiness and from Pleasure."[56] He remembers feeling this joy from a desire that was not satisfied, but it was more desirable to have desire than to have any other satisfaction—and this is the key to Romanticism. It is the joy that comes from a special kind of longing that is different from all other types of longings by a special characteristic:

[54] C. S. Lewis, *The Pilgrim's Regress* (London: Found Paperbacks, 1977), 10. The book was originally published in 1933, and this is from a preface added to the third edition of the book in 1943.
[55] Ibid., 12.
[56] Lewis, *Surprised by Joy*, 18.

In the first place, though the sense of want is acute and even painful, yet the mere wanting is felt to be somehow a delight. Other desires are felt as pleasures only if satisfaction is expected in the near future: hunger is pleasant only while we know (or believe) that we are soon going to eat. But this desire, even when there is no hope of possible satisfaction, continues to be prized, and even to be preferred to anything else in the world, by those who have once felt it. This hunger is better than any other fullness; this poverty better than all other wealth. And thus it comes about, that if the desire is long absent, it may itself be desired, and that new desiring becomes a new instance of the original desire.[57]

I summarize: (1) by Romanticism he means an experience in which the wanting is the delight; (2) the desire is preferred to anything else in the world; (3) in fact, if the desire fades away, then we desire the desire, which reawakens the original desire as a new instance.

Awakening Desire

Most people are mistaken when they match their desire to some particular object and think they could satisfy the desire by obtaining it. Every one of the supposed objects for the desire is inadequate to it. Here is a mature expression of this thought in *Mere Christianity*:

If I find in myself a desire which no experience in this world can satisfy, the most probable explanation is that I was made for another world. If none of my earthly pleasures satisfy it, that does not prove that the universe is a fraud. Probably earthly pleasures were never meant to satisfy it, but only to arouse it, to suggest the real thing.

[57] Lewis, *The Pilgrim's Regress*, 12.

If that is so, I must take care, on the one hand, never to despise, or be unthankful for, these earthly blessings, and on the other, never to mistake them for the something else of which they are only a kind of copy, or echo, or mirage. I must keep alive in myself the desire for my true country, which I shall not find till after death.[58]

Remember that we have already encountered this thought in Tolkien when he described fairy stories as being primarily concerned not with possibility, but with *desirability*. Lewis thinks we do not desire enough, or hard enough, or deep enough, or long enough: "It would seem that Our Lord finds our desires not too strong, but too weak. We are half-hearted creatures, fooling about with drink and sex and ambition when infinite joy is offered us, like an ignorant child who wants to go on making mud pies in a slum because he cannot imagine what is meant by the offer of a holiday at the sea. We are far too easily pleased."[59] If he could, Lewis would awaken desire in us. That is why we are drawn to Narnia, like steel to its lodestone.

Why fairy story in a children's book? Because it shows us our true country behind nature's curtain, the archetype behind the ectype. We call our desire for our true country by various names, Lewis says in his indispensable essay "The Weight of Glory," names like nostalgia or romanticism or beauty, and we pretend that settles the matter.

But all this is a cheat.... The books or the music in which we thought the beauty was located will betray us if we trust to them; it was not *in* them, it only came *through* them, and what came through them was longing.... For

[58] C.S. Lewis, *Mere Christianity* (San Francisco: Harper, 2009), 136–37.
[59] C.S. Lewis, "The Weight of Glory," in *The Weight of Glory* (San Francisco: HarperSanFrancisco, 2001), 26.

they are not the thing itself; they are only the scent of a flower we have not found, the echo of a tune we have not heard, news from a country we have never yet visited. Do you think I am trying to weave a spell? Perhaps I am; but remember your fairy tales. Spells are used for breaking enchantments as well as for inducing them. And you and I have need of the strongest spell that can be found to wake us from the evil enchantment of worldliness which has been laid upon us for nearly a hundred years. Almost our whole education has been directed to silencing this shy, persistent, inner voice; almost all our modern philosophies have been devised to convince us that the good of man is to be found on this earth.[60]

Narnia is enchanting because it disenchants us from worldliness.

Nature is prodigious, marvelous, stupendous. So "what more, you may ask, do we want?" Lewis wants to know. "We do not want merely to *see* beauty, though, God knows, even that is bounty enough. We want something else which can hardly be put into words—to be united with the beauty we see, to pass into it, to receive it into ourselves, to bathe in it, to become part of it."[61] That is what mythopoeia does, that is what fairy tales do, and that is what the subcreator of these children's stories has done: "We have peopled air and earth and water with gods and goddesses and nymphs and elves that, though we cannot, yet these projections can, enjoy in themselves that beauty, grace, and power of which Nature is the image. . . . We are summoned to pass in through Nature, beyond her, into that splendour which she fitfully reflects."[62]

[60] Ibid., 30–31.
[61] Ibid., 42.
[62] Ibid., 42–43.

In the chronicles, Lewis summons us to pass through our world into Narnia, then to pass through Narnia into the deeper country, which is our true home. Suppose—just suppose—a story carved in the hard stone of fairy tale (supposal literature) could facilitate such an expedition. That would be worth reading again. And carefully.

I

THE LION, THE WITCH
AND THE WARDROBE

On Knowing Him Here for a Little

A poem in seven parts

Madeline Infantine

> That was the very reason why you were brought to Narnia, that by knowing me here for a little, you may know me better there.
>
> —Aslan to Edmund and Lucy,
> *The Voyage of the "Dawn Treader"*

Part I

To know him here is to know the forest thaws:
the frigid sledge of death strikes stone,
its rider proud and cold and stern.

To feel the heart leap (and hardly know why)
as beech trees put forth delicate leaves.

Blue-crested kingfishers bow down in prayer,
while yellow-billed warblers belt ballads shared.
And—can you believe?
      Here is the song of the thrush.

Streams come chattering, splashing away frost,
brooks murmur to us: listen, watch.

Here is the dark green of the glad tree,
the sunlight of the celandines,
the festival of crocuses,
fresh moss, full thickets.

Where once was frozen silence, only song:
braying mare, yelping mouse,
barking hound, thumping beaver.

Come and see:
from his love, life
from his breath, spring.

You might find anything in a place like this.

The Power to Thaw Frozen Hearts:
The Lion, the Witch and the Wardrobe

Leonard J. DeLorenzo

Could you possibly imagine a better way to explain evil to children than to give them a figure who makes it always winter and never Christmas?

Those of us who live in northern climates know only too well that winter loses its charm when it goes on and on. Up north, when February turns to March, our hearts chill and shrink as we realize that "March" really means "Second February." Were every month from here on just to become another hidden February, we could easily imagine how soon we'd despair at the lost hope for spring. We'd burrow into our own little dens trying to keep a little corner of lingering warmth in a world grown so very cold.

Or maybe imagine London during World War II. The war is endless. The air raids are nearly constant. All the children are locked up inside, their parents locked inside with them, and it's becoming harder and harder to imagine anything else. Every day is more of the same. Always war and never holiday.

But what if four children do get out of London, out of the range of the constant bombardments? They're sent to live "in the heart of the country, ten miles from the nearest railway station and two miles from the nearest post office.''[1] Suddenly it seems like a holiday, right in the middle of war, and the countryside is their playground.

Except that, on the very first day of their newfound freedom, it starts to rain, forcing the children to huddle inside as drops fall from the sky. They find themselves doing just what they would be doing in London where other things fall from the sky.

At least here they are in a much larger house, one that is totally foreign to them, with lots of places to explore. If you've ever explored a new house—no matter how big or how unfamiliar—you know it is only a matter of time before the place starts to seem quite a bit smaller. You come to an end of exploring and soon enough it will feel like just another place that is boxing you in. I suppose that would be the case anywhere, in any old house, once the spark of adventure is doused, and wonder turns to boredom, and boredom turns to complacency, and complacency turns to resignation, and resignation does things to you: it makes you callous and bitter and cold inside.

That would be the case anywhere—except in a place where a new door to adventure suddenly appears. Not a door that leads into another room, or outside, or into some secret corner that you claim as your own. It would have to be a door that leads to another world.

And yet, wouldn't you know it—as you step out of the world where it's always war and never holiday, you find that this new world is a world where it's always winter and never Christmas.

What child, no matter how intrigued by this new adventure, doesn't immediately feel just how wrong that is? What child wouldn't want that kind of winter—in this new world that they've only been in for a moment—to come to an end? What child wouldn't feel the need to

[1] Lewis, *The Lion, the Witch and the Wardrobe*, 111, chap. 1.

hope for a better world in that strange world? It would become a different kind of playground: a battleground for the resiliency of hope.

The Children's World

Narnia is the children's world. It is not accessible to someone who is too much of an adult. And I, dear reader, am an adult.

That's why my five-year-old had to show me how to enter Narnia and how to understand it. That's why the most important things that I've seen there are the things I have seen through him. Only a child understands the children's world, so the key for adults is to become like children.

Lewis himself grasped this intuitively. Children pay closer attention to the concreteness of the story, yielding their minds and their imaginations to what they are hearing and what they are seeing. They are far less interested in standing at a distance to judge or analyze what is taking place; rather, they give themselves over to being drawn in, as Lewis explains:

> A child is always thinking about those details in a story which a grown-up regards as indifferent. If when you first told the tale your hero was warned by three little men appearing on the left of the road, and when you tell it again you introduce one little man on the right of the road, the child protests. And the child is right. You think it makes no difference because you are not living the story at all.[2]

[2] C. S. Lewis, "Hamlet: The Prince or the Poet?," in *Selected Literary Essays*, ed. Walter Hooper (Cambridge: Cambridge University Press, 1969), 104–5. I first came upon this passage in Michael Ward's *Planet Narnia: The Seven Heavens in the Imagination of C. S. Lewis* (New York: Oxford University Press, 2008), 18.

Lewis is praising the faculty of imagination. The child—
who is more inclined and willing to imagine—draws the
concrete image of the story before his mind's eye. At
the same time, he also allows the story to draw him in,
so that he inhabits this narrative space that becomes real
for him. There is, it seems, a kind of double displacement:
the story is displaced from the page and carried into the
child's imagination, and the child is displaced from his
world and carried into the story.

My (then) five-year-old, Isaac, is the one who really
felt what it means for it to be always winter and never
Christmas. He knew how to *read* this story, even though
he could not yet read when he first encountered it. He
only heard the story once when I read it to him, but it was
far more real to him that it was to me, not despite but precisely because of my grown-up-ness, my learning, and my
desire to be sophisticated. I was not ready to be displaced;
Isaac had to show me the beauty of doing so.[3]

Isaac cannot write a chapter like this; I can. What Isaac
could do that I was not prepared to do was really see this
story and inhabit it. That means that much of what I write
comes from how I learned to see something new through
how Isaac saw things.

[3] Tolkien cautions against making "grown-up" a bad word in opposition to
the good word of "child." As he rightly clarifies, "Children are meant to grow
up, and not to become Peter Pans. Not to lose innocence and wonder, but
to proceed on the appointed journey." "On Fairy-Stories," in *Tree and Leaf*
(London: HarperCollins, 2001), 45. Lewis' own view seems to rhyme with
this, though it also bears noting that, in a letter to a child named Marcia in
1955, Lewis says that being too "grown-up" is precisely how one loses interest
in Narnia: "Haven't you noticed that in the two [chronicles] you have read
that [Susan] is rather fond of being too grown-up. I am sorry to say that side of
her got stronger and she forgot about Narnia." *Letters to Children* (New York:
Macmillan, 1985), 51.

Lion Hunting

Isaac didn't know a single thing about C. S. Lewis when we cracked this book for the first time. He had no idea if Lewis had an "intention" when he started writing; five-year-olds do not think about authors' intentions. They just go into a story.[4]

How Isaac went into this particular story is, I believe, quite revelatory. It is revelatory of just how mischievous C. S. Lewis is. His mischievousness is right there on the title page since he titled the book: *The Lion, the Witch and the Wardrobe*. Those three things are listed in the reverse order that they appear in the story itself: first comes the wardrobe, then comes the Witch, and last of all—after quite a bit of time—the Lion. What Lewis did by naming the Lion first was make my son relentlessly curious about this Lion.

So we began. Chapter 1: no Lion. Chapter 2: no Lion. Chapter 3: no Lion. Chapters 4, 5, 6: no Lion. All the while Isaac just kept asking, "Where's the Lion?"

Seven chapters in—an eternity for a child—and there is the first mention of the Lion, though even then it isn't entirely clear to a child that we've found the Lion we're looking for. That's because what we get in chapter 7 is a name: "Aslan." The very sound of that name to a child totally new to this world—as my Isaac was—catches attention and stirs some wonder.[5] Isaac of "Where's the Lion?"

[4] Regarding Lewis' original "intention" in writing Narnia (or lack thereof), see his "Sometimes Fairy Stories May Say Best What's to Be Said," in *Of Other Worlds: Essays and Stories* (New York: Harcourt, 1994), especially page 36.

[5] This is reason enough to order the stories according to their publication order, rather than their chronological order within the narrative itself. The way of discovery is weakened when *The Lion, the Witch and the Wardrobe* comes second rather than first. Of course, Lewis himself may have preferred that the

suddenly focused very hard on this new question: "Who's Aslan?"

What happened to Isaac is the same thing that happens to the children (in chapter 7) as they walk with Mr. Beaver through Narnia: like them, Isaac felt quite different. I don't know how to explain this different feeling for Isaac because I'm not his author, but Lewis got to explain it for the Penvensies: "Edmund felt a sensation of mysterious horror. Peter felt suddenly brave and adventurous. Susan felt as if some delicious smell or some delightful strain of music had just floated by her. And Lucy got the feeling you have when you wake up in the morning and realize that it is the beginning of the holidays or the beginning of summer."[6] The feeling of holiday in the middle of war. The feeling of summer in the middle of winter.

C. S. Lewis is so mischievous. Even before the first word of the story, he's got children wondering about this Lion. It's not unlike how the very first snowflake gets children thinking immediately of the possibility of sledding and snow days, or how the end of Thanksgiving gets them thinking of Christmas, or how March makes us think in advance of spring—even if all other evidence is to the contrary. From the start, "the Lion" is associated with something natural in children: the hope for great things, even right in the middle of bleak things.

"Where's the Lion?"

---

chronicles be read in the chronological order of the narrative, though evidence on that point is far from conclusive. The most widely cited evidence for Lewis' preference for the chronological over publication order appears in a letter from 1957 to a child named Laurence, where Lewis sides with Laurence (who preferred the chronological order) rather than with the child's mother (who preferred the publication order). See *Letters to Children*, 68.

[6] *The Lion, the Witch and the Wardrobe*, 141, chap. 7.

A Land for Kings and Queens

That sparkle for adventure—the courage to peek out ahead to search for the thing you're eager to find even when you don't really know what that thing is[7]—is what gets this whole Narnian story moving in the first place. The Pevensie children were stuck inside on a rainy day but Peter—the oldest—is determined to go exploring. The others go along with him. There are a bunch of rooms. Some pictures and a suit of armor to see in one, a harp in the corner of another, a balcony off the end of a third. Then there was one sort of dull room—a spare room—with an uninspiring old wardrobe. There is nothing else in the room except a dead bluebottle on the windowsill: this room is a dead end.[8] Peter leads them out of that room, everyone follows him back the way they came—everyone except the youngest, Lucy.

The wardrobe has a door so she wants to try it. It opens and she walks through. She is careful not to shut the door behind her because—for reasons that are difficult to fathom—Lewis insists over and over again that it is a

[7] This seems to correspond with Lewis' meaning of "Joy." See especially *Surprised by Joy* (New York: Harcourt Brace, 1955), 18.

[8] In the 2005 film version of the story, Lucy looks to the window just before entering the wardrobe and sees the bluebottle buzz for a few seconds and then descend to its silent death. She looks away from the death scene toward the wardrobe. Ivan Head posits that here, even more than in the book, the dramatic connection to Emily Dickenson's poem about the death of a fly (and the end of seeing) is enacted. Entering the wardrobe is a kind of death, and in the land beyond that wardrobe, death will eventually bring those who love Aslan to the wideness of his own country. See Ivan Head, "Emily Dickinson in Narnia: The Buzzing Fly in the Room," *CASE*, June 1, 2006, https://www.case.edu.au/blogs/case-subscription-library/emily-dickinson-in-narnia-the-buzzing-fly-in-the-room.

very foolish thing to shut yourself into a wardrobe. That's apparently his one rule. He'd be an odd babysitter.

The next door Lucy walks through is at the back of the wardrobe, and it is not one she finds: it is one she's given. That is how one gets into Narnia—by surprise, as a gift. The snow that is suddenly making sound beneath her feet is the same snow she'll be standing on with her siblings the first time they hear the name Aslan sometime later. Did the Lion draw Lucy into Narnia? It would be hard to say that he did not.

This is how children enter into Narnia—every time. Some door or other appears, and both the appearance of the door and the invitation to pass through are always given without warning. It is just a sudden gift. What happens on the other side of that door is the story of that gift becoming a task—namely, the challenging task of learning to love Narnia on its own terms.

In Narnia, it really matters what you do, it really matters what kind of person you are, and it really matters what you are willing to become. Narnia, after all, is the children's world. This is a world that they are meant to rule. That is a responsibility that *cannot* be given to them. That is something they have to earn and desire. For the children who walk through that door to become capable of ruling Narnia, they must learn to love Narnia for what it is. They must grow into the kings and queens they are called to be.[9]

When the four Pevensie children first enter Narnia together, they are immediately presented according to who they are and who they are called to be. Peter apologizes to Lucy for not believing her about Narnia earlier. Lucy of course forgives him—because that's what Lucy does—then Peter, totally in character, says they must go

[9] See, again, Tolkien, "On Fairy-Stories," 45.

exploring. Susan, who is rather sensible, declares that it's cold. The sensible Susan suggests they put on the coats from the wardrobe. Peter doesn't want to take them because the coats aren't theirs, but Susan, who again is so sensible, says that technically they won't even be taking the coats out of the wardrobe, which settles things, in just the way the logic of children's games happens. And so we find this description of the four Penvensie children in their Narnian coats: "The coats were rather too big for them so that they came down to their heels and looked more like royal robes than coats when they had put them on. But they all felt a good deal warmer and each thought that the others looked better suited in their new getups and more suitable to the landscape."[10] As they enter Narnia, they are not yet suitable to the landscape. They put on these coats—which are really royal robes—and these do make each of *the children* themselves look better suited and more suitable to this place. But of course, they need to grow into the coats. That is their task: to grow into their regal robes.

Narnia, under the rule of the Witch's winter, has only slaves—everyone assigned to a small place. For the children, though, Narnia is a vocational land.[11] They must become what they are called to be. They have to fight for it, and bring warmth to a world grown weary of the cold: a world where right now it's always winter and never Christmas.

Narnia is not just the setting for the story; the story is about what Narnia is—what Narnia is to become—through

[10] *The Lion, the Witch and the Wardrobe*, 135, chap. 6.

[11] Compare this to what Catherine Cavadini observes in her chapter in this volume regarding the theme of "dominion" in both the creation account of Genesis 1 and the creation of Narnia in *The Magician's Nephew*. Anthony Pagliarini expands on this theme in his chapter on *The Last Battle*.

those who must grow into their kingships and queen-ships.[12] Narnia is their setting and Narnia is their prize. This is the story of the relationship of children to their world, of what children are called to make of the world, and of what the world is meant to call forth from children. Narnia is the children's world.

Family Dynamics

How does a child reading or listening to this story find his place in this new world? How does Narnia begin to matter to them? It happens through the children who are *in* the story: the Penvensies.

Once Peter received a sword and shield from Father Christmas in chapter 10, what had been likely for some time became definite: my son Isaac wanted to be Peter. He wanted to be the guy with the sword. This is guaranteed stuff.

Peter later fights a wolf to save his sister, and—believe me—that absolutely deepened the attraction. Isaac wants to slay beasts. He wants to be brave like Peter.

Peter, you'll recall, is the one who always wants to go exploring. He starts the exploration in the old house. He wants to push into the wintery land when they walk through the wardrobe. He is always ready to rush ahead, like his biblical namesake.[13] But when an older brother is in charge like that, we know what that can do to the

---

[12] On the demands and conditions of "true human kingliness" that Lewis attempts to sketch out in this chronicle and the ones to follow, see Ward, *Planet Narnia*, 68–69.

[13] For accounts of Simon Peter's boldness, even to a fault, see, for example, Matthew 26:35, John 18:10, and John 21:7.

younger brother. It can grate on him. Unless the older brother is especially thoughtful about the younger brother, the younger might well become bitter.

My Isaac is a younger brother, with *two* older brothers. The older brother, Peter, got the sword. The older brother, Peter, leads the way. The older brother, Peter, is to be the *High* King of Narnia. And the older brother, Peter, is quick-tempered with his younger brother, Edmund.

Next in age to Peter is Susan, who is so sensible, but also so quick to want to stop the adventure at the first sign of trouble, as when they discover that Mr. Tumnus is missing and that the Witch has taken him. Susan is the one who says there's no point in going on, there will be no fun here, that it's getting colder, and that there's nothing to eat. Susan says she wishes they'd never come. (A five-year-old is not likely to recognize those complaints as his own, which they *often* are: hungry, bored, etc.)

Meanwhile, there's Lucy, the first of the four to discover Narnia. She is the only one to have met Mr. Tumnus; she is certain in her conviction about the wickedness of the Witch: the one who makes it always winter and never Christmas. Lucy is desperate to help Mr. Tumnus.

So there's Peter who's every little boy's ideal. There's Susan who points out the risk and the stakes—and who complains. And there's Lucy who sees what's important.

And then there's that little brother, Edmund. He was the second of the four to enter Narnia and the first to be in a position to know for certain that Lucy was telling the truth when she said there was such a place. But he didn't back up Lucy—he did the opposite: he kept ridiculing her for making up stories even though he knew her story was true. He did it to hurt her, but he did it especially to protect his own little secret. His secret was that he was going to be made High King—not Peter—because he had

a pact with the Queen of Narnia, whom he deceived himself into not seeing as a Witch.

When the others find out that Edmund was lying and not
Lucy, Edmund is at first embarrassed but then defensive and
finally vindictive: "I'll pay you all out for this," he mutters
to himself, "you pack of stuck-up, self-satisfied prigs."[14]

It is not hard to figure this all out from the perspective
of my son Isaac. Whom is Isaac to like? Peter. Whom is he
to trust? Lucy. To whom is he to listen in order to know
what the dangers are? Susan. And whom is he to dislike
and distrust from the start? Edmund, the little brother.

The Perverse Sweetness

Narnia is the children's world, but is it the right place for
Edmund? Is Edmund right for Narnia? It appears not.

From the start Edmund enters into Narnia with wicked
intentions. He has seen Lucy going back into the wardrobe;
he follows her not for kinship or the sake of adventure but
because he is determined to ridicule her. Foolishly—oh so
foolishly—*he shuts the wardrobe door behind him*, the cardi-
nal sin in Lewis' moral universe.[15] But Edmund sees some
light and so goes toward the light, assuming that the wardrobe door has swung back open. The light, of course, is

---

[14] *The Lion, the Witch and the Wardrobe*, 135, chap. 6.

[15] Apparently, there is an actual reason for Lewis' rule: "When Lewis sent
Owen Barfield a draft of [the book], Barfield's wife Maud was concerned lest
children read the story and accidentally lock themselves inside a wardrobe.
Lewis took this cautionary note to heart and ended up adding five warnings to
[the book] about not closing the door and locking oneself in. After the story
was published, a little boy in Oxford took a hatchet and chopped a hole in the
back of a family wardrobe, hoping to find his own way into Narnia." David
C. Downing, *Into the Wardrobe: C. S. Lewis and the Narnia Chronicles* (San Francisco: Jossey-Bass, 2005), 35.

coming from the other end of the wardrobe, and Edmund finds himself in Narnia, quite unexpectedly and against his intentions. His intention was to ridicule Lucy for her silly story about such a silly place.

Did the Lion draw Edmund into Narnia? It seems that spite and cruelty did. He seems ill-fit to love this place or to become worthy of ruling this world. Yet the promise to reign is precisely what is offered to him. It is a promise sealed not with a kiss but with candy.

My Isaac already had a feeling about Edmund even before this younger brother stepped through the wardrobe. Isaac didn't like that nobody believed Lucy, but he especially didn't like that Edmund teased her. Isaac didn't think about Edmund's intentions when Edmund entered the wardrobe—Isaac doesn't think about characters' intentions. He just already felt a certain way about Edmund. It is important to recognize *this*: for Isaac, that he already had a feeling about Edmund; for us, that we know Edmund's intentions when he entered Narnia. Otherwise, we might end up thinking something like, "Whatever he ends up doing, it was the candy that made him do it." It's not at all that simple.

In his first, secret trip to Narnia, Edmund finds himself face-to-face with "a great lady, taller than any woman Edmund had ever seen.... She has a beautiful face, but it's proud and cold and stern."[16] He's stunned into immobility. She's harsh with him; he feels as if she is going to do something terrible to him, and then suddenly she changes her tone.

This "Queen of Narnia" draws him up into her sledge and wraps him in her mantle to keep him warm. She gives him something hot to drink, then asks what he would like

[16] *The Lion, the Witch and the Wardrobe*, 123, chap. 3.

to eat—anything at all. "Turkish Delight, please, your Majesty."[17] He receives several pounds of it. "The more he ate, the more he wanted to eat, and he never asked himself why the Queen should be so inquisitive."[18] She was very inquisitive about where he came from, and especially about the fact that he was one of *four* siblings.

Edmund finishes the *several pounds* of Turkish delight and just desperately wants more. That's when the Queen—who's really a witch—promises Edmund what he's supposed to become but in precisely the wrong way:

> I have no children of my own. I want a nice boy whom I could bring up as a Prince and who would be King of Narnia when I am gone. While he was Prince he would wear a gold crown and eat Turkish Delight all day long.... You are to be the Prince and—later on—the King; that is understood. But you must have courtiers and nobles. I will make your brother a Duke and your sisters Duchesses.[19]

The Witch is not feeding Edmund something poisonous from outside of him; she is leading him to feast on the poison within.[20]

That envy for his older brother, the pleasure he derives from putting his little sister down, that secret festering urge to upend them all and become better than them—that's Edmund's poison. It is as sweet as the candy he likes best, and he can easily gorge himself on more and more of it,

---

[17] Ibid., 125, chap. 4.

[18] Ibid.

[19] Ibid., 126, chap. 4.

[20] John C. Cavadini uncovers the meaning of "perverse sweetness" from Augustine in his essay "The Sweetness of the Word: Salvation and Rhetoric in Augustine's 'De Doctrina Christiana,'" in *Augustine's De Doctrina Christiana: A Classic of Western Culture*, ed. Duane Arnold and Pamela Bright (Notre Dame, IN: University of Notre Dame Press, 1995), especially 170.

always seeking after satisfaction but never quite finding himself full because he's still bitter. His hunger grows even as the sweet thing makes him ill: "He still wanted to taste that Turkish Delight again more than he wanted anything else.... He was already more than half on the side of the Witch."[21] The Witch is using the poison inside Edmund to lead him to seek his place as royalty and to enjoy the good of companionship in the wrong way.

The Queen enchants Edmund not only with the promise of superiority relative to his siblings, but also with the allure of joining up with her: "It would be fun to keep a secret between the two of us, wouldn't it?"[22] In his essay on what he calls "The Inner Ring," Lewis says that the drive of unhealthy ambition is not limited to the accrual of tangible profits like power, money, and the like. Instead, he says, "all these would not satisfy us if we did not get in addition the delicious sense of secret intimacy."[23] Lewis seems to have a moment like Edmund's in mind when he says of those tempted to overrule their conscience that "you will be drawn in, if you are drawn in, not by desire for gain or ease, but merely because at that moment, when the cup was so near your lips, you cannot bear to be thrust back again into the cold outer world."[24] Edmund wants to be "in," as most little brothers do.

Isaac could not name the "perverse sweetness." But Isaac did have a concrete feeling about Edmund. And he definitely didn't like the Witch. This whole thing is spoiled from the start. Isaac knows that. It seems like Edmund is all wrong for Narnia.

---

[21] *The Lion, the Witch and the Wardrobe*, 128, chap. 4.

[22] Ibid., 127, chap. 4.

[23] C. S. Lewis, "The Inner Ring," in *The Weight of Glory* (San Francisco: HarperCollins, 2001), 151.

[24] Ibid., 153.

The Stain of Treason

When Edmund finally does run away to the Witch's house, it is Mr. Beaver who says what every child has been feeling from the beginning: "The moment I set eyes on that brother of yours I said to myself 'Treacherous.' He had the look of one who has been with the Witch and eaten her food."[25]

Treacherous. Edmund is a traitor. What was his betrayal? He did of course slip away and run to the Witch, the very one who makes it *always winter and never Christmas*. He didn't quite complete the deed he was ordered to do, though, which was to bring his siblings with him to her castle. But he did go there to tell her where his siblings were, yet it wasn't because he wished them harm. It was more because he wanted to have authority over them. Peter, after all, could be a duke, so long as he, Edmund, were the King—he would be "in" with the Queen in a way that the others were not. That is the sweetness the Witch used to lure Edmund, and the root of his treachery.

Edmund's more complete betrayal, though, was against Lucy. It is a betrayal that happened early—in between Narnia and England. It was when Edmund turned the opportunity to back up his sister's story into the prime occasion to injure his sister. He did it out of spite. He did it because he wanted to protect his secret arrangement. He did it knowing full well that it would hurt Lucy, very badly. He did it. And so my Isaac did not like Edmund one bit. He liked Lucy, as he liked Peter.

All the same, Isaac started to worry about Edmund as it became clear that the Witch really did mean to hurt

---

[25] *The Lion, the Witch and the Wardrobe*, 149, chap. 8.

him. Actually, she meant to kill him. It was precisely when things are bleakest for Edmund that my Isaac was really worried about him—this Edmund who hurt Lucy.

Eventually, Edmund finds himself in the dark, closed in and surrounded by the Witch's cruel fiends. He's tied up under a tree—hungry, tired, and alone.[26] And here's the next passage:

> "Prepare the victim," said the Witch. And the dwarf undid Edmund's collar and folded back his shirt at the neck. Then he took Edmund's hair and pulled his head back so that he had to raise his chin. After that Edmund heard a strange noise—whizz—whizz—whizz. For a moment he couldn't think what it was. Then he realized. It was the sound of a knife being sharpened.[27]

It did not matter right then that Isaac had started out really not liking Edmund. When Edmund was tied up, with no way out, all closed in, Isaac found himself hoping for Edmund. Isaac was totally caught up in the story and yet not wanting it to keep going the way it was.

With the flurry of activity that immediately follows, it is hard for a child to follow along. I had to read it *twice* and then tell Isaac that Aslan's army saved Edmund from the Witch. Edmund was safe. Isaac was happy. The Penvensie siblings were also happy, even if they didn't have the words to express how they felt: "Edmund shook hands with each of the others and said to each of them in turn, 'I'm sorry,' and everyone said, 'That's all right.'"[28]

---

[26] Tirian, the last king of Narnia, will find himself in comparable circumstances. See *The Last Battle*, 687–89, chap. 4.

[27] *The Lion, the Witch and the Wardrobe*, 173, chap. 13.

[28] Ibid., 174, chap. 13.

By that point, Peter had already said a hard thing to Aslan when he first met the great Lion. He—Peter— confessed his own part in driving Edmund away, because of how he treated his younger brother. For her part, Lucy, whom Edmund injured most, had pleaded with Aslan to do something for Edmund. Now here he was: Aslan had brought their brother back—back from the edge of death and back from past the point of betrayal. And Edmund apologized. And they forgave him. And the family was whole again.

It is not hard to feel what the siblings feel: the relief of the moment. But this moment lasts hardly any time at all in the story. It is almost immediately disturbed. An emissary of the Witch has come into Aslan's camp. The Witch wants a word with Aslan.

Before we turn to why the Witch has come, I want us to think about what the siblings know, not necessarily as a matter of conscious cognition but rather in their very bones. Little brothers know what it's like to lash out, and they are expert in all the reasons for doing it. Older brothers and sisters know how to stir up their younger siblings. All siblings know how starting over is never a one-and-done sort of thing—how the next time your sibling does something to annoy you or even harm you, you can so easily go right back to drumming up all the old stuff. Coworkers know that, too. So do friends. So do spouses.

For these siblings—the three who were injured by the fourth—when the time comes that things go sour for them and they need someone close at hand to blame, can't you just imagine them saying or even just thinking, "You know, if not for our brother ..."?

That. That right there—that is part of the Witch's spell. The spell is not just about winter in Narnia; it is the chilling of hearts. It is not just about eliciting treason; it's about showing us to each other as traitors and remembering each other according to our sins.[29]

And so, sure enough, the Witch comes to Aslan's camp to remind them that there's a traitor there. And it's true; there is.

> Though it was bright sunshine everyone felt suddenly cold.... "You have a traitor there, Aslan," said the Witch. Of course everyone present knew that she meant Edmund. But Edmund had got past thinking about himself after all he'd been through and after the talk he'd had [with Aslan] that morning. He just went on looking at Aslan. It didn't seem to matter what the Witch said.[30]

It does not matter to Edmund what the Witch says, but it does matter to his siblings. Aslan had told them there was no need to talk about what was past but at the very mention of a "traitor," they think of their brother. What is past is past for Edmund; not, so it seems, for them. They've forgiven him, but he is still the one who betrayed them. How do you undo *that* spell? How do you dig out that thought sunk deep into their hearts, a thought that is in danger of permanently darkening the way they see their brother?

The Meaning of Sacrifice

Does Aslan die for Edmund's sin? The Witch does have rights to Edmund's life, according to the deep magic of

[29] The last act of the devil is to accuse the saints of their sins. The triumph of the devil would be for the saints to believe in those accusations more than they trust in the blood that has healed them and redeemed their memories. This also means healing and redeeming their memories of each other. See Revelation 12:10.

[30] *The Lion, the Witch and the Wardrobe*, 175, chap. 13.

Narnia. What is that deep magic? Is it some cruel, high, unbending rule? Is it the honor of the Emperor-beyond-the-Sea? We don't quite know. I don't think we are supposed to know—not from Lewis, anyway.[31]

I find myself thinking about Edmund having no idea at first that the Witch has come for him, that *he* is the traitor in their midst. He's just looking at Aslan. Whatever Aslan said to him, whatever Aslan already did for him, changed the way he thought about himself. He starts seeing himself through Aslan.

I find myself thinking about his siblings, too. I think about them thinking about Edmund. They wish he were not the traitor they each *know* that he is.

It does not seem very likely that Lucy would be the one plagued by dislike or suspicion for Edmund, at some point later, if he showed signs of his old self. But then again, she was the one he hurt the worst, and a wound inflicted by a loved one brings the worst kind of trauma. Then there's Susan, who is fairly punctilious—she *is* the kind of person who would likely remember Edmund's folly. And no doubt Peter would be subject to demeaning Edmund when brothers fight, as they do. And even Isaac—my Isaac—who did not like Edmund one bit at the beginning, could probably very easily learn to not like him again at the first sign of doubt.

So who needs saving? Is it Edmund? I suppose, in the sense that his life hangs in the balance. But isn't it also his siblings, whose memories of their brother are wounded even though they've forgiven him?

Aslan and the Witch move out of earshot. When Aslan turns around, he announces that the Witch has renounced

[31] Peter Schakel offers a helpful bit of commentary on this deep magic in *Is Your Lord Large Enough? How C. S. Lewis Expands Our View of God* (Downers Grove, IL: InterVarsity Press, 2008), 54.

her claim to Edmund's blood. He gives no explanation as to why or how—it is simply done. Oddly, do you know who's not mentioned again until three full chapters later? Edmund.

In the following scene, Aslan instructs Peter how to lead the army in battle when the Witch attacks, as he fully expects she will. Then Aslan separates himself, eventually moving away under the cover of darkness while Lucy and Susan follow at a distance. Peter, who saw Aslan confer with the Witch to save his brother's life, is now consumed with preparing for battle. The next time we'll hear from him, he will be the one speaking of Edmund. But again, that's three chapters later. In the interim, we go with the girls to see Aslan's end of the bargain.

Lucy and Susan watch as Aslan gives himself over to his enemies. They bind him. They shave his glorious mane. They muzzle him. They mock him. They bind him tighter. They lay him upon the stone table. "The children did not see the actual moment of the killing. They couldn't bear to look and had covered their eyes."[32] But it happened.

It happens well out of sight of Peter and the others. They do not know what has happened, that *this* happened. They are busy readying themselves for battle. And Lucy and Susan, who are there when *this* happened, are not there when the Witch attacks Peter and the others, as Aslan knew she would. Peter is in one scene; the girls are in the other.

Those who have read the story and who therefore somehow stand above it already know and see that Aslan returns. Even if we, as grown-ups, are new to the story, we likely already sense how Aslan is being presented, and so we more than half expect that his death will be overcome,

---

[32] *The Lion, the Witch and the Wardrobe*, 181, chap. 14.

that he'll rise. And he does. That's the way this story goes, after all. I'll want to bring us back to this "knowledge" of ours in just a moment. But for now, let's just know what we know—Aslan is raised. Then after he brings the final thaw upon Narnia in breathing life upon the frozen statues in the Witch's court, he races with Lucy and Susan back to Peter and the others, who are engaged in battle with the Witch.

By the time Aslan and the others arrive at the battlefield, Peter's army is few in number but still engaged, fighting with all its might. Peter himself is fighting the Witch, who is *not* holding her wand. She only has her stone knife. With her wand, Peter would have been turned to stone and the battle would have already been lost. But without the wand, Peter was able to hold his own against the Witch as he fought at the head of his army *for* Narnia. Aslan will finish what Peter started: he slays the Witch.

How did they fend off the Witch without Aslan? Peter tells the tale: "It was all Edmund's doing, Aslan.... We'd have been beaten if it hadn't been for him. The Witch was turning our troops into stone right and left. But nothing would stop him.... He had the sense to bring his sword smashing down on her wand.... Once her wand was broken we began to have some chance—if we hadn't lost so many already. He was terribly wounded. We must go and see him."[33] Edmund. It was Edmund. Edmund with wisdom and bravery attacked the Witch in the only way that would work: by first depriving her of her magic. He went right after the magic that once enchanted him. It wounded him greatly, but he fought her who sentenced him to being *always a traitor and never a brother.* In Edmund,

[33] Ibid., 192, chap. 17.

the sacrifice of Aslan caused contrition, then sacrifice. This is not just imitation; this is the manifestation of a new man. Edmund fought to undo his own treachery.

At the stone table, the girls saw the sacrifice; on the battlefield, Peter saw the fruit. What it cost was Aslan's life. What it won was Edmund's own sacrifice. Aslan saved Edmund and Edmund fought to save Narnia. The girls saw one part, Peter saw the other—they were each witnesses, in their own way. Peter *praises* his little brother.[34] Lucy *heals* the one who wounded her.[35] That's what Aslan did for *them*, even though none of them saw to the depths of what he did.

A couple months after we finished the story, I asked my son Isaac a few questions.

"Isaac, what did you think about Edmund when he lied about Lucy?"

"I didn't like him."

"Did you like him at the end after Aslan brought him back?"

"I guess so."

"Do you remember what he did in the battle?"

"He broke the Witch's wand—and got really hurt."

"What did you think about that?"

"I wanted to be like Edmund."

Isaac always wanted to be like Peter. Peter's the one who got the sword from Father Christmas, and Peter's the one who killed the wolf who was attacking his sister. In the end, not only Peter is praising Edmund; Isaac is. Aslan redeemed Edmund in Peter's eyes—and in Isaac's.

So who does Aslan die for?

---

[34] As Cain and the elder brother in the parable would not do. See Genesis 4:1–16 and Luke 15:25–32, respectively.

[35] As the patriarch Joseph would do for his brothers who left him for dead. See Genesis 45:1–28.

68

How It All Works

Thinking too much about "how" Aslan's sacrifice works is a very bad thing to do. Here is what I mean: it has become fashionable for some theologians to want to think so much about "how" the sacrifice of Christ works that they become dissatisfied with the answers they find and end up saying there really wasn't a sacrifice at all, or at least not a need for it.[36] The true tragedy is that those who analyze too much and who want to peek behind the mystery, in the vain attempt to show that no one needed to die for our sins, miss the only thing that really matters: the fact that someone did.

That's all stuff that my five-year-old son does not *think* about. But let me tell you what happened to him when I read these parts of the story to him. He could not believe that Aslan was killed. He thought he *couldn't* be dead; it couldn't be *Aslan*. He asked who that Lion was. He just couldn't believe it. I had to tell him that Aslan was dead. The look in his eye I won't soon forget.

We who know so much are a little too wise to "a motif" here, but Lewis claims that "concrete imagination" knows nothing of such things.[37] We—who become

---

[36] A notable recent example comes from the theologian Elizabeth Johnson. For a brief presentation of her view, see Elizabeth Johnson, "No One Had to Die for Our Sins," *U.S. Catholic*, November 27, 2018, https://uscatholic.org /articles/201811/no-one-had-to-die-for-our-sins/. Khaled Anatolios argues against the eclipse of atonement in modern theologies and the related preoccupation with "models" of salvation in his *Deification through the Cross* (Grand Rapids, MI: Eerdmans, 2020). We might very well consider Lewis' own words about approaching God and seeking to understand: "The ancient man approached God (or even the gods) as the accused person approaches his judge. For the modern man the roles are reversed. He is the judge: God is in the dock." C. S. Lewis, "God in the Dock," in *The Collected Works of C. S. Lewis* (New York: Inspirational, 1996), 464.

[37] Lewis, "Hamlet: The Prince or the Poet?," 105.

"grown-up"—probably already expected something very much like what happened to happen: Aslan would rise. It is sad that we *expect* that, because I will perhaps *never* forget the surprise, the gasp, the joy when Isaac heard these words: "There, shining in the sunrise, larger than they had seen him before, shaking his mane ... stood Aslan himself."[38]

There is something like an explanation that soon follows within the story, about deeper magic that goes back before the dawn of time, in which a willing and spotless victim could take the place of a traitor and then death itself would start working backward.[39] Isaac did not care one iota about the explanation. All that mattered was that Aslan was alive. And that is what matters to Lucy and Susan.[40]

Lewis does not overly concern himself with a "theory of atonement"; he presents us with the *fact* of atonement. We can lose the fact for the sake of a theory. Lewis gave us the better part.[41]

---

[38] *The Lion, the Witch and the Wardrobe*, 184, chap. 15. During the "Fourth Week" of Saint Ignatius of Loyola's Spiritual Exercises—the week devoted to the Resurrection—the exercitant is to beg for the grace to "be glad and rejoice intensely." It is a striking petition: to ask to be glad and rejoice. Joy, it seems, is a divine gift. A child like Isaac was ready for this grace at Aslan's rising. See Ignatius of Loyola, *The Spiritual Exercises of Saint Ignatius*, ed. and trans. Louis J. Puhl (Chicago: Loyola Press, [2021]), no. 221.

[39] Compare Lewis' discussion of miracles, nature, and the "revelations of that total harmony of all that exists" in *Miracles: A Preliminary Study* (New York: HarperOne, 2001), 97–98.

[40] I find Lewis' conclusive statement about Jesus Christ to be apropos here: " 'What are we to make of Christ?' There is no question of what we can make of Him, it is entirely a question of what He intends to make of us. You must accept or reject the story." "What Are We to Make of Jesus Christ?," in *Collected Works of Lewis*, 407).

[41] Michael Ward puts the matter this way: "The Narnian atonement is a means to an end, not an end in itself.... Lewis is not so much interested in how the atonement worked as in the fact that it worked.... At some point, we must simply Enjoy it as one feature of divine life ... to taste it." *Planet Narnia*, 70.

The First to Love Him

Aslan's sacrifice is the greatest gift that the children receive: by his sacrifice they are empowered to save and cherish Narnia as its kings and queens—together. Aslan warms Narnia; his approach is the arrival of spring. His breath revives the stone statues in the Witch's courtyard. Everyone receives new life from the action of Aslan. But there is one child who seems to live by Aslan's power from the very beginning. That, of course, is Lucy.

On her first trip into Narnia, Lucy meets the faun Tumnus at the lamppost. He invites her into his den, for tea. She goes willingly, spritely. She is, as Tumnus says, the "Daughter of Eve from the far land of Spare Oom *where eternal summer reigns.*"[42]

The two of them have a really wonderful tea, complete with all kinds of pleasant (British) foods. The faun tells her stories. Then he plays a flute for her that makes her want to "cry and laugh and dance and go to sleep all at the same time."[43] She does fall asleep, and when she stirs awake, the mood has changed.

By the signs of friendship, the faun drew her in. By the appearance of hospitality, he made her comfortable. By the sound of his song, he meant to keep her there, so that he could find the Witch and betray this child to her, under whose pay he himself is confined. That's how he kept a little warmth for himself in a world where it was always winter and never Christmas.

It is completely to Tumnus' advantage to give the Witch what she wants. It is completely at a risk to himself that he would do otherwise. Nevertheless, he will not

---

[42] *The Lion, the Witch and the Wardrobe*, 116, chap. 2 (italics added).
[43] Ibid., 117, chap. 2.

follow through with the treason that began under the false pretenses of friendship. Why? Because he'd never actually met a human before, and Lucy is not what he expected we would be like. She is kind. She is trusting. She is warmth itself. She seems to come from a place where eternal *summer* reigns. She *is* summer in the middle of winter.

Tumnus did deceive her, he did mean her harm, and he did act for himself alone. Even when he decides to break off his treachery, he is still overcome with the shame of it—he is ashamed of what he meant to do.

> "C-can you ever forgive me for what I meant to do?" said the Faun.
> "Why, of course I can," said Lucy.[44]

Because that's what Lucy does. She forgives. She heals. She warms. Aslan will bring spring to all of Narnia, but already from the start Lucy lives by Aslan's power.

Behold, Lucy the Valiant—who has the power to thaw frozen hearts. She is the Queen of Narnia who did *not* shut the wardrobe door. That would have been *very foolish*. She was always meant to come back. Because Narnia is the children's world, and what they learn in that world they bring back through to warm our world that has become unnaturally cold.[45]

[44] Ibid., 119, chap. 2.

[45] Lewis' description of how joy suddenly melted what he describes as his "long winter" at the outset of the period of his early life he calls his "Renaissance" is tellingly reminiscent of the way Narnia is warmed by Aslan and, in alliance with him, by Lucy and the others. See *Surprised by Joy*, 72.

II

PRINCE CASPIAN

On Knowing Him Here for a Little

Part II

Madeline Infantine

To know him is to know him when you see him
or to doubt—and see nothing at all.

To hear his call, by night, and wake with trembling
below the moon, below the wild stars.

His is the dear voice, the call heard
in the still wood, where trees forget
how to dance.

To know him is to wake the others,
to face their grumbling, sleepy sulking—
                              to be thought a liar.

Knowing him is trusting him
at the dark edge
of the cliffside night
and following over the precipice
down the gorge
blind on the stone-shrouded path.

To know him is to know him when you see him
or to fear the woods, quiet

the call, forget to be
brave.

Seen or unseen, he is
leading the sleepy, the shaky-legged, and the
breathless.

The Hard Virtue of *Prince Caspian*

Michael Ward

A successful spiritual journey through *Prince Caspian* requires that we understand the spiritual symbol that it embodies and expresses. As I have argued elsewhere,[1] C. S. Lewis constructed the Chronicles of Narnia so that they should embody and express the spiritual symbols of the seven heavens. John Donne called these heavens "the Heptarchy, the seven kingdoms of the seven planets."[2] Lewis said this about them: "The characters of the planets, as conceived by medieval astrology, seem to me to have a permanent value as spiritual symbols—to provide a *Phänomenologie des Geistes* which is especially worthwhile in our own generation."[3]

This is no small claim. The seven heavens, in Lewis' view, are not an outdated curiosity fit only for superstitious, prescientific, medieval minds; on the contrary, they have a permanent and ongoing role to play in the human imagination, and a value that was of particular worth in his own day. This is why he spends so much time in various works informing his readers of the seven planets and their

---

[1] *Planet Narnia: The Seven Heavens in the Imagination of C. S. Lewis* (New York: Oxford University Press, 2008). The present essay is derived in part from chapter four of *Planet Narnia*.

[2] John Donne, *Donne's Sermons: Selected Passages with an Essay by Logan Pearsall Smith* (Oxford: Clarendon, 1919), 160.

[3] "The Alliterative Metre," in *Selected Literary Essays*, ed. Walter Hooper (Cambridge: Cambridge University Press, 1969), 24.

characteristic qualities. In "The Heavens" (chapter 5 of
The Discarded Image), in "The Descent of the Gods" (chapter 15 of *That Hideous Strength*), and in "The Planets" (a
long, complicated, alliterative poem that he published in
1935), Lewis attempts to revive these spiritual archetypes
for his contemporaries. In the Chronicles of Narnia, he
continues that effort, but this time implicitly, tacitly, not
telling us what he is up to, but throwing us, as it were,
blindfolded into seven different imaginative creations,
each of them infused with and informed by one of these
heptarchical symbols.

    Prince Caspian embodies and expresses the spiritual sym-
bol of Mars, and we will only properly understand the
spirituality of this chronicle if, first, we grasp Lewis' overall
communicative strategy in expressing the planetary symbols through implicit means and, second, grasp his tactical
deployment of the symbol of Mars in this particular tale.
In *An Experiment in Criticism*, Lewis maintains that every
work of literary art can be analyzed under two heads, both
as something made (*poiema*), a work of poetic skill, and as
something said (*logos*), a work with a message. Many readers of the chronicles jump straight to the *logos*; they want
to know "what Lewis is saying," what his "point" is. But
we must not be hasty. We must not exchange the poetry
of the chronicles for a pot of message. The *logos* of each
tale is inextricably bound up with the *poiema*, and only if
we attune our literary antennae to the artistic and archi-
tectonic skill with which Lewis constructed each chronicle
can we hope to discern its message successfully. Once we
comprehend both Lewis' general objectives in the Narniad
as a whole and their peculiar outworkings in this story,
we will be well placed to hear what *Prince Caspian* has to
say. We must be "attentive and obedient," making sure of
our imaginative "orders" before we draw any conclusions

about the book's message. That is how we intelligently "receive" rather than merely "use" the literature that Lewis has put before us.[4]

Implicit Communication

Lewis once told his friend George Sayer that he was interested in the "atmosphere" of each of the Narnia chronicles,[5] and this atmospheric quality is a very important category to have in mind if we are to get the best out of the books. In his essay "On Stories" Lewis writes: "To be stories at all stories must be series of events. But it must be understood that this series—the *plot*, as we call it—is only really a net whereby to catch something else. The real theme may be, and perhaps usually is, something that has no sequence in it, something other than a process and much more like a state or a quality."[6]

The qualitative tone or flavor is the main reason why we reread our favorite stories many times in the course of our lives. If it were just the plot that we were interested in, we probably would not read a story more than once. Why would you want to read it again unless you had forgotten what happened? But with your favorite novels you revisit them many times.

Take a great novel like *Pride and Prejudice*. You might well read it on numerous occasions in the course of your life, not because you have forgotten (spoiler alert!) that

[4] C. S. Lewis, *An Experiment in Criticism* (Cambridge: Cambridge University Press, 1961), 34, 19.

[5] George Sayer, *Jack: C. S. Lewis and His Times* (San Francisco: Harper and Row, 1988), 191.

[6] "On Stories," in *Of Other Worlds: Essays and Stories* (New York: Harcourt, 1994), 18.

Elizabeth Bennet marries Mr. Darcy, but because you like the Austen world; you appreciate what might be called the "Austentatious" flavor of the imaginative space to which her novels provide access. But with a lesser kind of novel, such as a standard whodunit murder mystery (a typical Agatha Christie, for example), where there's not much more than a clever plot, you tend not to reread, unless you have forgotten who did the murder, because Agatha Christie doesn't provide her readers with much in the way of atmospherics or three-dimensionality.

Lewis maintains that "a story of this kind [a fairy tale or romance] is in a way more like a symphony than a novel.... It is always the symphonic treatment of the images that counts, the combination that makes out of them a poetic whole."[7] And a poetic whole is just that: poetic and whole. A great writer establishes the "tone" or "key" of a story not only by creating each and every part with great care, but by creating all the *relationships* between those parts with great care. Only as we, the readers, receive the work holistically, understanding the parts and the whole and the way the whole interrelates with the parts, will we be able properly to appreciate the story in hand.

The interesting thing about this sort of literary atmosphere is that it is not located in any particular thing (such as the main character or the dominant theme or the climactic scene) but has to be read off the warp and woof of the entire text. We need to discern the total flavor or tone of each chronicle, its pervasive atmosphere, a qualitative value that is related to and to an extent dependent on, but not identical with, the individual component parts.

Lewis achieves this atmospheric quality by an ingenious development of a literary technique he called "transferred

---

[7] C.S. Lewis, *Spenser's Images of Life*, ed. Alastair Fowler (Cambridge: Cambridge University Press, 1967), 116–17.

classicism." In a review of *The Oxford Book of Christian Verse*, Lewis points out that writers—Christian writers—in the Middle Ages and Renaissance would often reach back into the classical past and ransack the myths of ancient Greece and Rome in order to obtain certain imaginative materials that they would then deploy for Christian purposes. They would seize upon any number of classical deities—Zeus, Jupiter, Apollo, Venus, whoever it may be—and they would transfer those characters into their Christian art. In this way, God—the Christian God—will often appear in medieval or Renaissance literature, but disguised, incognito, masked behind a veil of superficially pagan characteristics. Everybody is in on the secret, of course; everybody knows that these pagan gods have been stripped of their divinity and are now serving ancillary roles in Christian poetry. The classical gods and goddesses now symbolize aspects of the true God, and this is the best means, Lewis says, by which literature can be religious without being devotional.

Transferred classicism baptizes classical mythology and turns it to Christian effect. It's similar to what we find Saint Paul doing in the Acts of the Apostles. Preaching to the men of Athens on the Areopagus (or Mars Hill, as the Romans called it), Paul says, "[God] is not far from each one of us, for 'In him we live and move and have our being'; as even some of your poets have said, 'For we are indeed his offspring'" (Acts 17:27–28). Paul is quoting here two ancient Greek poems about Zeus: one by Epimenides, one by Aratus. In context, these pagan poets had written that it is "in Zeus we live and move and have our being," for "we are indeed Zeus's offspring." Of course, Saint Paul isn't encouraging the men of Athens to worship Zeus. He is using Zeus as a springboard into his own presentation of the gospel. He is saying, as it were, "You're right that we live and move and have our being in God, and you're right that we're God's offspring, but you're wrong in calling him Zeus; he is in fact the God and Father of our Lord Jesus Christ." It's an early kind of transferred classicism.

With both biblical and a medieval precedent before him, then, Lewis had no hesitation in taking the planetary gods and goddesses—the tutelary spirits of the seven heavens—and exploiting them poetically in the Narnia chronicles. But what is *un*precedented about Lewis' deployment of "transferred classicism" is that he uses it to accomplish two things simultaneously. On the one hand, he is concerned with an all-pervasive atmosphere or tone; on the other hand, he is portraying the Christian God. He deploys his chosen planetary character to achieve both aims at once.

Here we need to take a step back and clarify what is meant by "the Christian God." The Christian revelation of God can be summed up in the phrase "the Word became flesh" (John 1:14). God's Word, who creates all things and sustains all things, becomes human in the person of Jesus. But in becoming incarnate, the divine Word does not cease being the creative principle and the sustaining power behind all things. "All things" are not suddenly evacuated of the divine presence that they signify. On the contrary, that divine presence is brought to a new pitch of perceptibility.

Lewis was interested in these verses from the Letter to the Colossians: "For in him all things were created ... and in him all things hold together" (Col 1:16–17). He was sufficiently interested in these words to paraphrase them in one of his books. He paraphrases them thus: "Christ is the all-pervasive principle of concretion or cohesion whereby the universe holds together."[8] He also once remarked that the whole Narnia series was "about Christ."[9] When we hear

---

[8] *Miracles: A Preliminary Study* (New York: HarperOne, 2001), 121.

[9] Letter to Anne Jenkins (5 March 1961), in *The Collected Letters of C. S. Lewis*, ed. Walter Hooper (London: HarperCollins, 2004–2007), 3:1244.

that Narnia is "about Christ," we immediately think of
Aslan, the Christ character who does Christlike things:
who dies for Edmund in *The Lion, the Witch and the Wardrobe*; who brings Narnia to birth in *The Magician's Nephew*;
who judges Narnia in *The Last Battle*. The Christological
parallels in those three books are very clear and obvious;
you can't miss them. It's less immediately clear how Aslan
represents elements of Christ's life and ministry in the other
four. But if we think of Christology more in the cosmic
sense as indicated in the Letter to the Colossians, then we
may be getting closer to Lewis' meaning when he says that
the whole Narnia series is "about Christ." We shouldn't
just be looking for hard-and-fast, one-to-one parallels
between what Aslan does in Narnia and what Jesus does in
the Bible. We should be thinking more holistically, more
cosmically. We should be asking ourselves how Lewis
would go about depicting an "all-pervasive principle of
concretion or cohesion." That would be a much harder
thing to put into a story than a simple "Christ figure" who
does Christlike things, but it would be equally part of biblical Christology. It would also comport with Lewis' stated
intention of being concerned with "the atmosphere" of
the chronicles. It would suggest that we should expect a
kind of harmony or resonance between the Christ character and the cosmos that he inhabits, between Aslan himself
and his Narnian kingdom, in each chronicle—naturally so,
for the same Word is to be heard sounding in both.

"Martianity"

One other preliminary provisional matter that we need to
address before we get to *Prince Caspian* is a very quick trot
through Lewis' lifelong interest in Mars-related, or Martial, symbolism.

Lewis was only about five or six years old when, according to Walter Hooper, he wrote a story, an incomplete story, titled "To Mars and Back," set in the fictional world of Boxen. It exists in two pages of Lewis' immature handwriting and is published in the first edition of *C. S. Lewis: Images of His World*. This is the earliest evidence of his interest in Mars and all things chivalric, gallant, and knightly. His Boxen juvenilia feature a character called Samuel Macgoullah, who is a chess knight come to life. Jumping ahead a decade to Lewis' midteens, we find him enraptured by Chaucer's "Knight's Tale," which he considers "a perfect poem of chivalry."[10] He would later remark approvingly upon how "the character and influence of the planets are worked into the *Knight's Tale*."[11] By this he means, among other things, that the climax of Chaucer's poem happens, appropriately enough, on a Tuesday, the day of Mars. To the Spanish, Tuesday is *Martes*, and to the French, *Mardi*. In English we name the day by reference to the Norse equivalent of Mars, Tyr or Tiw. Lewis writes of Tyr, whose hand was bitten off by a wolf, in his poem "A Cliché Came out of Its Cage."

While still a teenager, Lewis gained firsthand experience of what it would mean in the modern day to be armed and drilled, if not as a knight then at least as a second lieutenant. On his nineteenth birthday he arrived in the trenches of France, having been given a commission as a junior officer in the British army. He served for about six months and later described this frontline service as "an odious necessity."[12] "Necessity" is an interesting term. In his poem "The Planets," he portrays Mars as "cold and

---

[10] *They Stand Together: The Letters of C. S Lewis to Arthur Greeves*, ed. Walter Hooper (London: Collins, 1979), 104.

[11] *The Discarded Image* (Cambridge: Cambridge University Press, 1964), 198.

[12] *Surprised by Joy* (New York: Harcourt Brace, 1955), 151.

strong, / Necessity's son."[13] During the Second World
War, he would write an article entitled "The Necessity
of Chivalry," in which he argued that the knightly ideal is
vital if we are to avoid a world "divided between wolves
who do not understand, and sheep who cannot defend,
the things which make life desirable."[14]

But we get ahead of ourselves. Shortly before the out-
break of the Second World War, Lewis published his first
novel, *Out of the Silent Planet* (1938), which is set (where else
but?) on Mars. The unfinished story that he wrote as a boy,
"To Mars and Back," finally achieved public form in this first
volume of a trilogy of interplanetary adventures. He names
Mars "Malacandra" and locates most of the story there. The
planet, however, is not just the setting for the story; the
Martial spirit is also part and parcel of the drama. Following
the arrival on Malacandra of the protagonist, Elwin Ransom, every incident and image is designed to contribute
to and help communicate this Martial spirit, for, as Lewis
asks, "What's the excuse for locating one's story on Mars
unless 'Martianity' is through & through *used*?... Emotion-
ally & atmospherically *as well as* logically."[15] Thus Ransom
becomes increasingly Martial as the story progresses. We
are told that "something in the air he now breathed"[16] was
making him strengthen and become a man, a hunter. He is
frightened before he participates in the hunt for the *hnakra*,
the monster that lives in the water, but the hunt "was necessary, and the necessary was always possible."[17]

[13] *Collected Poems of C. S. Lewis*, ed. Walter Hooper (London: HarperCollins,
1994), 27–28.

[14] "The Necessity of Chivalry," in *Essay Collection: Faith, Christianity, and the
Church*, ed. Lesley Walmsley (London: HarperCollins, 2000), 720.

[15] Letter to Arthur C. Clarke (20 January 1954), in *Collected Letters of Lewis*,
3:412.

[16] *Out of the Silent Planet* (New York: Scribner, 2003), 79.

[17] Ibid.

Before leaving *Out of the Silent Planet*, we should notice one other recurrent image throughout the story, and that is the trees, the forest. On Malacandra there are ancient woods that have now been turned to stone. One of the Malacandran races lives in the forest lowlands, another lives surrounded by forests, and a third race is likened to trees. Ransom comes across "such trees as man had never seen," and so on and so forth. All these references to trees are not accidental, but are part and parcel of the planet's presiding spirit. Lewis is drawing on his classical education. In Roman mythology, Mars was not always and only the god of war; he was originally a vegetation deity, associated with trees and forests and known as Mars Silvanus—and thus distinguished from Mars Gradivus, the god more specifically responsible for overseeing military matters. Mars was the springtime divinity, a pagan belief still echoing in the fact that the third month of the year, March, is so named. March is sacred to Mars because in that period of the year, the trees come back to life after winter and kings march off to war as the weather becomes warmer and more suited to battle. Lewis would have known all this from Cato the Elder and from Frazer's *Golden Bough*, among other sources.

In the third volume of the Ransom Trilogy, *That Hideous Strength*, the planetary characters actually come down to Earth to bring about the denouement of the whole story. When the spirit of Malacandra descends upon Ransom and upon Merlin (the medieval wizard newly arrived in the twentieth century), Lewis writes:

> Something tonic and lusty and cheerily cold, like a sea breeze, was coming over them. There was no fear anywhere: the blood inside them flowed as if to a marching-song. They felt themselves taking their places in the ordered rhythm of the universe, side by side with punctual

seasons and patterned atoms and the obeying Seraphim. Under the immense weight of their obedience their wills stood up straight and untiring like caryatids. Eased of all fickleness and all protestings they stood: gay, light, nimble, and alert. They had outlived all anxieties; care was a word without meaning. To live meant to share in this processional pomp. Ransom knew, as a man knows when he touches iron, the clear, taut splendour of that celestial spirit which now flashed between them: vigilant Malacandra, captain of a cold orb, whom men call Mars and Mavors, and Tyr who put his hand in the wolf-mouth.[18]

In this powerful passage, Lewis is attempting to convey, as he puts it in a letter to a friend, "the *good* element in the martial spirit," what he calls "the discipline and freedom from anxiety" that come from surrendering to the military chain of command.[19] The Martial influence can, of course, be put to bad effect, hence the "brutal and ferocious" elements that he found in Gustav Holst's musical portrayal of the Martial spirit in his suite *The Planets*, a piece of music that Lewis knew and greatly admired.

The mention of iron reminds us that each of the planets was associated with a different metal. Writing of Mars in his poem "The Planets," Lewis describes "His metal's iron / That was hammered through hands into holy cross."[20] And the connection between Mars and Christ's crucifixion brings us to one last remaining Martial influence that we should comment on before turning to *Prince Caspian*. The male protagonist of *That Hideous Strength* is one Mark Studdock. As his first name indicates, Mark has a special connection with Mars. We learn that Mark

---

[18] *That Hideous Strength*, reprint edition (New York: Scribner, 2003), 336.
[19] Letter to Sister Penelope (31 January 1946), in *Collected Letters of Lewis*, 2:702.
[20] *Collected Poems of Lewis*, 27–28.

"had never seen war,"[21] but he is to be tried in his own personal battle as the story progresses. The villains of the story are determined to bring Mark to that state of subjugation wherein obedience to the devilish purposes of the National Institute for Co-ordinated Experiments (N.I.C.E.) is, ever afterwards, "a matter of psychological, or even physical, necessity."[22] Mark had in childhood imagined himself as a "hero and martyr," and he now realizes he's facing a "straight fight" and is about to find out the truth of his childhood fancies. He finds that this prospect, after the long series of diplomatic failures that he's gone through, acts as a "tonic." (Note that word again.) The crucial moment comes when Mark is required by the villains of the N.I.C.E. to trample upon a crucifix. As he looks down at the crucified form of Christ, "thinking hard," the defenseless wooden figure on the cross, nailed and helpless, becomes for him a picture of what happens "when the Straight met the Crooked."[23] Mark decides to remain straight; he refuses to join the crooked side. He stands in witness to something of which he's not quite sure yet—namely an objectively real value outside himself and his own immediate interests. It is the *"experimentum crucis"* (the crucial experiment, the critical test) of which Lewis had written in *The Abolition of Man*.[24] It is not an explicit conversion to Christianity, but it is a moment of truth for Mark, as he witnesses to the goodness (the "Straightness") of Christ. And having become a witness, he has become, quite literally, a martyr, for that is what the word means. Admittedly, he is only a "white martyr." He doesn't actually die, or even shed his blood, but he is a martyr nevertheless. Dante in the *Paradiso* assigns martyrs to the sphere

[21] *That Hideous Strength*, 219.

[22] Ibid., 348.

[23] Ibid.

[24] *The Abolition of Man* (San Francisco: HarperCollins, 2001), 30.

of Mars—partly, Lewis says in *The Discarded Image*, because of the obvious connection that martyrs usually die a violent death, but also, he says, because of a mistaken philological connection between *martyr* and *Martem*.

"Martial Policy"

Lewis had brought his Ransom trilogy to its conclusion, but his involvement with things Martial was far from over. In his second Chronicle of Narnia, *Prince Caspian*, he returns to this theme he first tackled when he was five or six years old, taking the four Pevensie children, as it were, to Mars and back. To Narnia and back, yes, but Narnia as imagined through a Martial lens.

How interesting that an early scene in *Prince Caspian* involves the planets! Doctor Cornelius takes the young Caspian up the tower at night and shows him the conjunction of Tarva and Alambil, a conjunction interpreted by Glenstorm the centaur as betokening some great good for the sad realm of Narnia. The stars foretell success if the old Narnians who live in hiding emerge and try to overturn the usurper Miraz. So *Prince Caspian* is a war story; it's the "civil war" of Narnia, as Lewis elsewhere describes it—"the great war of Deliverance" as it's called in the timeline of Narnian history. It's interesting how the very word "martial" itself appears more than once in this story but never again in any of the other Narnia books. Reepicheep is described as a "gay and martial mouse."[25] He is

[25] *Prince Caspian*, 352, chap. 6. The word "martial" appears twice and the word "marshal" appears seven times in *Prince Caspian*; neither word appears even once in any of the other chronicles. The word "arms" (in the sense of weapons) occurs more often in *Prince Caspian* than in any other Narnian tale and is doubtless an anagrammatical nod to "Mars." George Herbert, whose poetry Lewis greatly admired, puns on "army" and "Mary" in "The Temple"

gay, light, nimble, and alert, rather like that effect Malacandra has as he comes down on Earth at the end of the
Ransom trilogy. Miraz, the usurper, frets over his "martial
policy" and in something of a pun, or, as one might say,
a "mistaken philological connection," we have the "mar-
shals" of the lists overseeing the single combat.[26]

Very clearly, then, *Prince Caspian* is a war story, a Martial story. Let us quickly survey some of the more obvious
militaristic happenings in the story. The children redis-
cover their armor in the treasury beneath the ruins of Cair
Paravel. Trumpkin is taken to his death by two Telmarine
soldiers but rescued by the four Pevensies as they see him
struggling in the boat. Once Trumpkin is rescued, he is
put to two tests: a swordsmanship test with Edmund and
an archery test with Susan. Caspian himself, having escaped
from the castle of his uncle, is found by the old Narnians
who live in hiding and is advised by Glenstorm the centaur
to summon a "council of war." The rebellion commences.
The Old Narnians skirmish with the occupying forces, and
the Pevensie children with Trumpkin become involved. A
notable moment occurs in Aslan's How, where Caspian is
attacked by a werewolf and is bitten in the hand, in a way
reminiscent of the Norse god Tyr.

Because Caspian is injured, he is unable to enter the
single combat, the "monomachy" as it is described. Therefore Peter fights Miraz on Caspian's behalf, but we should
note that Peter does not actually succeed in defeating
Miraz. Rather, Miraz is stabbed in the back by one of his

("How well her name an *Army* doth present / In whom the Lord of Hosts did
pitch his tent"), and I suspect that Lewis is subtly making a similar discreet
wordplay here.

[26] A marshal literally is one who has responsibility for governing *mares*,
horses. It was originally a term in horsemanship, with no explicit connection
to the planet Mars.

own men, indicating how the Telmarines are very far from being truly Martial: they have no discipline or order or self-control. And the interesting thing is that Miraz himself seems to recognize this. At any rate, even as he frets over his "martial policy," he scorns his courtiers for being "lily-livered,"[27] drawing on the tradition of medieval thought that assigned virtues to certain bodily organs. The liver was believed to be the seat of courage, and a truly Martial liver would give warriors "stomach," as Shakespeare's Henry V puts it ("He which hath no stomach to this fight, / Let him depart"). The Telmarine armed forces are morally anemic, insufficiently hardened by the iron of Mars.

Hardness is a key term in Lewis' Martial lexicon. Mars produces "sturdy hardiness"[28] and the Martial visage is "hard and happy," according to his poem "The Planets." This "hard virtue of Mars"[29] appears frequently throughout *Prince Caspian*. Peter looks "hard" at Lucy; the soldiers escorting Trumpkin have faces that are "bearded and hard"; we meet three badgers called the "Hardbiters"; when the children are lost in the woods after failing to follow Aslan, they find that retracing their steps was "hard work, but oddly enough everyone felt more cheerful"; Peter's army at the end of the battle are found "breathing hard ... with stern and glad faces." Most significantly of all, Caspian begins "to harden" as he sleeps "under the stars."[30]

Caspian's hardness is tested in an interesting way when Peter steps in to fight on his behalf in the single combat. Caspian is the rightful king of Narnia, and from one

[27] *Prince Caspian*, 401, chap. 13.

[28] *The Discarded Image: An Introduction to Medieval and Renaissance Literature* (Cambridge: Cambridge University Press, 1964), 106.

[29] *Collected Poems of Lewis*, 59.

[30] *Prince Caspian*, chap. 7.

point of view, he ought to be the one to fight the usurper, Miraz. Indeed, he asks to do it and protests that he wishes to avenge the death of his own father. However, he has to accept the truth in Peter's statement that Miraz thinks he is just "a kid" and would therefore laugh at any challenge he issued. Further, he has to accept that Peter, as High King, has a certain authority over him and has come to Narnia not "to take your place, you know, but to put you into it." In other words, Caspian has to accept a chain of command and the rule of law, two key elements of the good Martial spirit. Regretfully, but obediently, he acknowledges the necessity of the situation when he would rather, if given his own way, have won back his throne through his own might, not through right mediated to him by Peter. But this very humility is what demonstrates the validity of his claim to kingship. Aslan asks him later, "Do you feel yourself sufficient to take up the Kingship of Narnia?" To which Caspian replies, "I—I don't think I do, Sir. I'm only a kid." "Good," says Aslan. "If you had felt yourself sufficient, it would have been a proof that you were not. Therefore, under us and under the High King, you shall be King of Narnia."[31]

It is Peter, therefore, who gets to fight the single combat with Miraz, a combat we should note that is witnessed not just by crowds of Narnians and Telmarines cheering on their own man, but also by a gathering host of tree spirits, the dryads, hamadryads, and—significantly—*sylvans*.

Only in this chronicle are the tree spirits ever called sylvans, and that is because Lewis is here glancing at the other aspect of his chosen Martial symbolism: Mars Silvanus, god of trees and forests. Mars, as we noted above, was not always and only the god of war; he was originally a vegetation deity. *Prince Caspian*, likewise, is not just a war

---

[31] Ibid., 411, chap. 15.

story but also an arboreal adventure. Caspian is knocked off his horse by a falling tree. When the Pevensie children are first deposited in Narnia, they find themselves in a woody place; they can hardly get out for all the branches and twigs that are poking into them. They find Narnia has been overgrown by trees and ivy, and they're told that the Telmarines are frightened of the forests. Lucy tries to wake the trees twice. The first time she fails but the second time, when Aslan is present, the trees do indeed begin to dance, and later on in the story there is a positively bacchanalian romp, as Bacchus and Silenus join in the revelry. Early in the book, we also hear about Pomona, the goddess of fruit trees and orchards.

In summary, then, Lewis structures *Prince Caspian* out of both military elements and arboreal elements because the whole book is designed to communicate the spirit of Mars. It is a truly Martial story, and having spent so much time attempting to understand the chronicle in its capacity as *poiema* (something made), we are now well placed to understand it in its capacity as *logos* (something said). Let us turn to address the spiritual significance of this Martial symbolism.

"It is hard for you, little one"

Perhaps the most obvious message conveyed by the means of this Martial *poiema* is what Lewis communicates explicitly in *Mere Christianity*, where he says that the idea of the knight, a Christian in arms for the defense of a good cause, is one of the great Christian ideas. Writing in the aftermath of a war that had threatened his country with Nazi rule, Lewis had obvious reason to champion this tradition of gallantry. In *Prince Caspian*, he is attempting to acquaint us and indeed delight us with what it feels like to live

inside that chivalric tradition. He's attempting to provide
his readers with imaginative access to the discipline and
freedom from anxiety that arise out of participation in the
Martial spirit. Deliverance by means of war is apparently
an unavoidable necessity. Peaceful protest isn't going to
get them anywhere because Narnia has degenerated into a
tyranny under Miraz.

Mars is "necessity's son," yes. But elsewhere Lewis
remarks that necessity was always "the tyrant's plea." He
is there quoting Milton, but the same sentiment is to be
found in Livy and Oliver Cromwell and William Pitt, all
of whom observed that the claim of necessity could always
be used by politicians to excuse any kind of behavior,
however brutal and cruel. Knowing this, how did Lewis
hope to make out that the necessity of his "war of Deliverance" could be anything other than a tyrannical evil itself?
Abusus non tollit usum. That was a Latin tag Lewis liked:
"Abuse does not abolish use." Just because tyrants may
falsely claim that necessity excuses cruelty and brutality
doesn't mean that there is never any such thing as a just
war. For Lewis, as for Saint Augustine, whose thoughts on
just war Lewis quotes to a correspondent, the weapons of
war could sometimes be legitimately wielded if real and
honest necessity arose.

But how to characterize real necessity? Lewis wishes to
call it the "Necessity of Chivalry," the title of an essay he
wrote in the dark days of August 1940, as Britain faced
the imminent threat of invasion. He argues that if Britain
is to avoid Nazi tyranny, it must have chivalrous soldiers
who, like Theseus in "The Knight's Tale," know how
to make a "virtue of necessity." The knightly ideal of the
Middle Ages brought together two things that have no
natural tendency to gravitate toward one another. The
knight, Lewis says, is a man of blood and iron, but also a

gentle, modest, unobtrusive man. The knight is fierce to nth degree but also meek to the nth degree—he combines both characters. And to Lewis, this knightly ideal wasn't an outdated curio but a living reality, practical and vital. He was no less admiring of it in his adulthood than he had been as a boy when he first was acquainted with Chaucer's tale. Some of Lewis' contemporaries, the Royal Air Force pilots, "to whom we owe our life from hour to hour," were the modern equivalents of the medieval knight. And their successors must be bred up if we are to escape from a world, as he puts it, divided between "wolves who do not understand, and sheep who cannot defend, the things which make life desirable."

Martial hardness is not to be confused with heartlessness. This kind of "hardness" might be best rendered in modern English as "tough love." It is the strength which, on the one hand, gives backbone to the milksop and, on the other hand, reins in machismo. Mars may be hard, but hardness is not necessarily cruelty. Mars is gentle without being weak, strong without being cruel. Within these parameters of the Martial spirit, war service, if it is truly necessary, may be entered into (as Lewis puts it in *Mere Christianity*) with "a kind of gaiety and wholeheartedness."[32] Gaiety, again—note that term.

It is this unashamed wholeheartedness that may explain why some critics think they have found in Narnia a glorification of conflict and retribution, a legitimizing of cruelty. Lewis would undoubtedly respond by saying that his critics have mistaken the abuse of the Martial spirit for its use. He believed there was a proper place for duly retributive justice and for just war. Indeed, he even went on the offensive in one place, addressing the Oxford Pacifist

---

[32] *Mere Christianity* (San Francisco: Harper, 2009), 119.

Society in 1940 with a speech titled "Why I Am Not a
Pacifist."[33] The chivalrous knight who risks life and limb
for the sake of the oppressed richly deserves to be hon-
ored. And if this honor happens to be easily corrupted
by propagandizing politicians, so what? Abuse does not
abolish use.

Lewis, however, would have rebutted with vigor the
allegation that his Narnian Martial spirit glorifies and legit-
imizes cruelty. Chivalry imposes crucial restraints on the
practice of war, so as to avoid violence that is not strictly
necessary. *Prince Caspian* memorably depicts this principle. Nikabrik, embittered by long suffering, is prepared
to employ even a hag and a werewolf to achieve his war
aims, for the ends justify the means, in his view. That kind
of unrestrained warring spirit Lewis regarded as completely
unacceptable, which is why he has Nikabrik come to a bad
end. He tries to avoid a jingoistic tone in other places too.
Peter in the single combat, we're told, is fearful; he doesn't
just go to it without a second thought. Edmund, remember, gets all choked up when he thinks that Peter might die
in this single combat. There is no gloating over the victims: Peter averts his eyes from the corpses of his enemies,
and he determines to honor even the traitor Nikabrik with
appropriate burial.

Lewis divided poets of war into three classes: the
enchanted, the disenchanted, and the re-enchanted. The
enchanted include Sir Philip Sidney, Thomas Babington
Macaulay, G. K. Chesterton, and Rupert Brooke; the disenchanted include Siegfried Sassoon; and the re-enchanted

[33] "Why I Am Not a Pacifist," in *Essay Collection: Faith, Christianity, and the
Church*, 281–93. Pacifist Stanley Hauerwas interacts with Lewis' thinking about
just war in his essay "On Violence," in *The Cambridge Companion to C. S. Lewis*,
ed. Robert MacSwain and Michael Ward (Cambridge: Cambridge University
Press, 2010).

are those such as Homer and the anonymous author of
"The Battle of Maldon." No doubt Lewis means to include
himself too among the re-enchanted. He says, "One is
not in the least deceived [about war]: we remember the
trenches too well. We know how much of the reality the
romantic view left out. But we also know that heroism
is a real thing."[34] So he aims to strike a balance between
propaganda on the one hand and protest on the other. No
doubt, chivalry is a failure, but it is not such a failure as
pacifism.[35] Wars, even just wars, inevitably involve evil,
but not so much evil as is involved in passively allowing
aggressors to have their way. For evil to triumph, it is only
necessary that good men do nothing.

In his magnum opus on English literature in the sixteenth century, he sums up these views by stating, "We
have discovered that the scheme of outlawing war has
made war more like an outlaw without making it less
frequent, and that to banish the knight does not alleviate
the suffering of the peasant."[36] The plight of the suffering
peasantry in Narnia, that is to say, the old Narnians who
live in hiding, *is* alleviated. It is alleviated by Aslan's great
thundering war cry in chapter 11, for here, at last, the Narnian Mars summons his troops to battle:

> Aslan, who seemed larger than before, lifted his head,
> shook his mane, and roared.
>   The sound, deep and throbbing at first like an organ
> beginning on a low note, rose and became louder, and
> then far louder again, till the earth and air were shaking

[34] "Talking about Bicycles," in *Essay Collection: Faith, Christianity, and the Church*, 691.
[35] See *English Literature in the Sixteenth Century, Excluding Drama* (Oxford: Clarendon, 1954), 153.
[36] Ibid.

with it. It rose up from that hill and floated across all Narnia. Down in Miraz's camp men woke, stared palely in one another's faces, and grasped their weapons. Down below that in the Great River, now at its coldest hour, the heads and shoulders of the nymphs, and the great weedy-bearded head of the river-god, rose from the water. Beyond it, in every field and wood, the alert ears of rabbits rose from their holes, the sleepy heads of birds came out from under wings, owls hooted, vixens barked, hedgehogs grunted, the trees stirred.[37]

This is Aslan's most obviously militaristic moment in the story, but one that has been prepared for in any number of ways before this moment. Aslan is clearly the commander in chief, who requires Lucy's absolute obedience, who takes the boys' salute, who instructs Peter to knight Caspian. He is the Narnian lord of hosts, mighty in battle, and the children in the story must grow up into his Martial spirit. Tarva, the Lord of Victory, is shedding his influence from the heavens. Sleeping on "hard" ground and breathing "the air of Narnia," Edmund toughens up: "All his old battles came back to him." The same "magic in the air" has saved Susan's bowstring from perishing, so that she too can play her part. Everything is present and ready for them to live into this new Martial reality—if only they will obey.

Obedience is not shown to be easy. It's a frightening demand that Aslan makes, especially upon Lucy, who must witness to the others in her party. Even though she's the youngest, Lucy has to go and wake all of them up in the middle of the night and tell them that they've been going in the wrong direction and that they must follow her immediately, and if they won't follow her, she'll go alone. Aslan acknowledges her difficulty, saying to her gently,

---

[37] *Prince Caspian*, 387, chap. 11.

"It is hard for you, little one." But though it is hard, it is necessary. This is the moment of truth for Lucy Pevensie. "It is a terrible thing to have to wake four people, all older than yourself and all very tired, for the purpose of telling them something they probably won't believe and making them do something they certainly won't like. 'I mustn't think about it, I must just do it,' thought Lucy."[38] And that is the turning point in the story. Lucy does her duty. She becomes a true spiritual warrior. She faithfully witnesses to what she's seen, and as a result, she turns the company about so that eventually even Susan can receive the Martial spirit. Susan had initially been very reluctant to see Aslan, but gradually she becomes more susceptible to the Martial spirit, taking Mars' "weight of obedience" on her shoulders.

> "You have listened to fears, child," said Aslan. "Come, let me breathe on you. Forget them. Are you brave again?"
> "A little, Aslan," said Susan.[39]

And in addition to this militaristic aspect of the Martial influence, the sylvan aspect asserts itself as the trees begin to participate more and more in the spirit of Aslan:

> Pale birch-girls were tossing their heads, willow-women pushed back their hair from their brooding faces to gaze on Aslan, the queenly beeches stood still and adored him, shaggy oak-men, lean and melancholy elms, shock-headed hollies ... and gay rowans, all bowed and rose again, shouting, "Aslan! Aslan!" in their various husky or creaking or wave-like voices.[40]

[38] Ibid., 381, chap. 10.
[39] Ibid., 386, chap. 11.
[40] Ibid., 388, chap. 11.

The trees of the field clap their hands even as the children put on the whole armor of God and fight the good fight. For Aslan is the *true* Mars, according to that technique of transferred classicism by means of which pagan gods could serve Christian purposes. The children grow up into the spirit of Aslan, the Martial spirit, because it surrounds them. In every part of Narnia, not just in the Christ character but in the whole Narnian universe as it is depicted in this story, Mars is shedding his influence abroad. For "[God] is not far from each one of us, for 'In him we live and move and have our being'; as even some of your poets have said, 'For we are indeed his offspring'" (Acts 17:27–28). The boys harden into the knights, the girls romp in the bacchanalian revelry with the swaying trees and the growing vines, and even seemingly unimportant little details like the discovery of the chess piece in the ruins of Cair Paravel at the start of the story contribute to the total effect. Of course, it has to be a chess *knight*. It couldn't be a chess pawn or a chess king or a chess bishop. *Everything* in this story is conspiring to generate the appropriate Martial atmosphere.[41]

In his single combat with Miraz, Peter does not make sufficient use of his shield. Lewis there, I think, is glancing at the "shield of faith" (Eph 6:16), by means of which the Christian may "put foreign armies to flight" (Heb

---

[41] As Katherine Langrish has argued, the chess piece is derived from "the Icelandic tale *The Deluding of Gylfi* which tells how after the days of Ragnarok and the destruction of the Norse gods, the Aesir, a fresh green earth will rise from the sea. Baldur will return from death and the sons of the gods will sit in peace, talking together about hidden wisdom and remembering the past: 'Then they will find there in the grass the golden chessmen the Aesir used to own ...' In their new, changed world, the chessmen are the last scanty evidence of a race of vanished gods and heroes, and here in Narnia the same applies." Katherine Langrish, *From Spare Oom to War Drobe: Travels in Narnia with My Nine-Year-Old Self* (London: Darton, Longman and Todd, 2021), 135–36.

11:34). Lewis refers to those scriptural sources elsewhere when discussing the ideal knight of faith. Faithful obedience is the chief virtue that Aslan imparts to his followers under the aegis of Mars in this story. It is a virtue of which George MacDonald had written, in a passage that Lewis anthologized:

> Do you ask, "What is faith in Him?" I answer, the leaving of your own way, your objects, your self, and the taking of His and Him ... *and doing as He tells you.* I can find no words strong enough to serve for the weight of this necessity—this obedience.[42]

Discipline, faithfulness, obedience, strength, growth— it's this spectrum of qualities that becomes available to those characters who are properly disposed to the Martial influence, to the Christological influence depicted by means of Mars that is showered upon them in this story. These characters steadily and increasingly enjoy the Martial influence that Aslan both incarnate and discarnate sheds abroad in this tale. Mars, we might even say, is the "unknown god" of *Prince Caspian* who surrounds and upholds Lucy and the others, forging them into warriors or woodlanders or witnesses or a mixture of all three. As the apostle Paul had once stood on the Areopagus and proclaimed to the men of Athens the person of Jesus Christ "in whom we live and move and have our being," so, in the second Chronicle of Narnia, Lewis does something very similar from his own Mars Hill.

---

[42] George MacDonald, *Unspoken Sermons* (New York: Cosimo Classics, 2007), 267 (quoted in Lewis' volume *George MacDonald*).

III

THE VOYAGE OF THE "DAWN TREADER"

On Knowing Him Here for a Little

Part III

Madeline Infantine

In the dark
hollow, dry
but for the moonlight
pool, asleep
in the shadows
with a hoarding
greedy heart—
        can you know him here?

Will you find
jewel-crammed pockets
emptied, sore scaly loneliness
cured?

His is the claw that tears us deep, undressing
the thick dark scales to fit us
for new clothes (not a tame salve).

To know him here is to shed the snakeskin,
to swim in the font, a child again.

Come, bathed and undragoned, as the sunrise
comes over the mountains and the bay
is the color of roses.

Come, smooth and soft, into the morning
where lilies lie on bright sweet water.

To know him is to learn to tell the story:
I was thick-scaled, then peeled,
not by my might, but by his.

The New Directions of
The Voyage of the "Dawn Treader"

Peter J. Schakel

"There was a boy called Eustace Clarence Scrubb, and he almost deserved it."[1] This is the opening sentence of C. S. Lewis' story *The Voyage of the "Dawn Treader"*—and one of the best opening lines ever. Such opening lines make you want to read on; the rest of the book has got to be good.

The Voyage of the "Dawn Treader" is the third book in a series of seven chronicles, but the opening lines of the two previous books are less memorable. Do you recall the first sentence of the first book, *The Lion, the Witch and the Wardrobe*? "Once there were four children whose names were Peter, Susan, Edmund and Lucy."[2] Not exactly an attention grabber, is it? If you didn't get that one, do you remember the opening sentence of the second one, *Prince Caspian*? "Once there were four children whose names were Peter, Susan, Edmund, and Lucy."[3] Not exactly original, is it?

The first sentence of *The Voyage of the "Dawn Treader"* perhaps signals that in this book Lewis was making a new beginning. He sets off in some new directions, and he experiments with some new possibilities and approaches, working with humor, social satire, and myth. That is a bit

[1] *The Voyage of the "Dawn Treader,"* 425, chap. 1.
[2] *The Lion, the Witch and the Wardrobe*, 111, chap. 1.
[3] *Prince Caspian*, 317, chap. 1.

surprising, because Lewis thought this would be the last book on Narnia that he would write. At least, that's what he said in a letter to eleven-year-old Laurence Krieg in 1957: "When I wrote *The Lion* I did not know I was going to write any more. Then I wrote *P. Caspian* as a sequel and still didn't think there would be any more, and when I had done the *Voyage* I felt quite sure it would be the last."[4] His experiments with new elements and techniques in *The Voyage of the "Dawn Treader"* may have had the welcome but unintended effect of making Lewis want to pursue these new directions further and thus want to write even more books about Narnia.

If we are going to look at the development of the Chronicles of Narnia, however, we need to clarify the order in which the books were written. This is somewhat complicated, because the original arrangement of the books has been changed by publishers over time. *The Lion, the Witch and the Wardrobe* was written first and published first and was generally considered book one once there were enough books to constitute a series. After *The Magician's Nephew*—which is set before the others chronologically—was published, it began to be regarded by some readers as book one. Likewise, *The Horse and His Boy*, though written and published fifth, was read in the number three slot—and so on. This arrangement was solidified in the 1994 HarperCollins edition of the Narnia series, in order to have readers encounter events in chronological order.

I think renumbering the chronicles, making *The Magician's Nephew* number one, was a mistake. As every storyteller knows, a good story does not depend on strict chronological presentation. *The Lion, the Witch and the Wardrobe* was conceived in Lewis' imagination as an

---

[4] C. S. Lewis, *Letters to Children* (New York: Macmillan, 1985), 68.

introduction to Narnia; it uses important strategies appropriate for a first book. Those strategies lose their full effects if the book is not read first. The best example of this is when Mr. Beaver first mentions the name Aslan and the narrator says, "None of the children knew who Aslan was any more than you do; but the moment the Beaver had spoken these words everyone felt quite different."[5] That carefully crafted sentence loses its wonder and mystery, as well as its effectiveness in drawing in readers to identify with the characters, if the reader has already gone through *The Magician's Nephew* and already learned about Aslan.[6]

First New Direction: Humor

Keeping in mind the original order in which the Chronicles of Narnia were written and published, let us take a look at the new directions Lewis followed in *The Voyage of the "Dawn Treader,"* starting with the use of humor. Lewis had a wonderful sense of humor. Richard Ladborough, a close friend when he and Lewis were colleagues at Cambridge University, remembered him as "jovial," a man who "delighted not only in hearing funny stories but also in telling them, and in this he was an expert."[7] Lewis' stepson Douglas Gresham remarks on "his enormous humor and [the] vibrancy of his wit.... You couldn't be

[5] *The Lion, the Witch and the Wardrobe*, 141, chap. 7.

[6] For a full discussion of the best order for reading the books, see Peter J. Schakel, *Imagination and the Arts in C. S. Lewis* (Columbia, MO: University of Missouri Press, 2002), 40–52; Peter J. Schakel, *The Way into Narnia: A Reader's Guide* (Grand Rapids: Eerdmans, 2005), 13–21.

[7] Richard W. Ladborough, "In Cambridge," in *C. S. Lewis at the Breakfast Table and Other Reminiscences*, ed. James T. Como (New York: Macmillan, 1979), 99.

with Jack for more than five or ten minutes without roaring with laughter."[8]

Humor is readily apparent in two of Lewis' earlier books, *The Screwtape Letters* and *The Great Divorce*, but there isn't much humor in *The Lion, the Witch and the Wardrobe*. The statement that in Narnia it is "always winter and never Christmas"[9] is amusing and memorable; it makes readers want to read on, the way the opening sentence of *The Voyage of the "Dawn Treader"* does. But it's sad, not funny. In *Prince Caspian*, chapter 4, the author of the book that Doctor Cornelius uses to teach grammar to the prince is named *Pulverulentus Siccus*,[10] Latin for "dry as dust." It's a pleasing example of academic wit. But most children wouldn't catch the humor, and nowadays few adults would either.

All of that changes with the opening sentence of *The Voyage of the "Dawn Treader."* Lewis seems to be trying something different in this book, right from the start. And the humor continues throughout the book. It shows up in Eustace's confrontations with a sword-wielding mouse, and it emerges in Eustace's diary entries, for example, in his comments on the ship itself, calling the *Dawn Treader* a "rotten little thing." "No proper saloon, no radio, no bathrooms, no deck-chairs," he continues. "I tried to tell [Caspian] what real ships are like, but he's too dense."[11]

There is also the wonderful comedy of the Dufflepuds, who agree about everything and toss out conversation stoppers like "What I always say is, when a chap's hungry, he likes some victuals" and "Getting dark now; always does

---

[8] Ginny McCabe, "'The Lion, the Witch and the Wardrobe' Will Capture Hearts and Imaginations of People Everywhere," *Across Pacific Magazine*, August 11, 2005, http://across.co.nz/LionWitchWardrobe05.html.

[9] *The Lion, the Witch and the Wardrobe*, 118, chap. 2.

[10] *Prince Caspian*, 337, chap. 4.

[11] *The Voyage of the "Dawn Treader,"* 437, chap. 2.

at night" and "Ah, you've come over the water. Powerful wet stuff, ain't it?"[12] Readers laugh at this, and so do the other characters—the Magician and Lucy laugh till tears run down their cheeks as they watch the Duffers hop about, relishing the fast one they pulled on the Magician: "Visible we are.... And what I say is, when chaps are visible, why they can see one another."[13] Here is a strain that is new to the series, a new way to make the book enjoyable, one that continues to be an appealing feature in the later books.

Humor continues to play a role in *The Horse and His Boy*, starting with the horse Bree's comment to the boy Shasta as they plan their escape from slavery: "You can't get very far on those two silly legs of yours (what absurd legs humans have!)."[14] Later, Shasta laughs as he watches Bree have a refreshing roll in the grass. There's the ironic humor of the only traffic regulation in the city of Tashbaan being "that everyone who is less important has to get out of the way for everyone who is more important."[15] And in a scene that children love, there is the moment when the Calormene prince Rabadash's armor gets caught on a hook and Rabadash is left dangling "like a piece of washing hung up to dry," before turning into a donkey.[16]

One could argue that Lewis' skill as a humorist improves from book to book. While much of the comedy in *Dawn Treader* and *The Horse and His Boy* is verbal, more likely to be effective with adults than with children, the humor in *The Silver Chair* begins to be suited to young readers. Kids love it when the hearing-impaired Trumpkin garbles what Jill and the owl try to communicate to him:

[12] Ibid., 492, chap. 10.
[13] Ibid., 502, chap. 11.
[14] *The Horse and His Boy*, 209, chap. 1.
[15] Ibid., 230, chap. 4.
[16] Ibid., 295, chap. 13, 307–8, chap. 15.

"The girl's called Jill," said the Owl, as loud as it could.

"What's that?" said the Dwarf. "The girls are all killed! I don't believe a word of it."[17]

Then there is Puddleglum the Marsh-wiggle, not only funny in appearance—his very long legs and arms and very short body, his "greeny-gray" hair ("if it can be called hair"), his pointed hat with an enormous brim, the smoke of his pipe tobacco creeping along the ground—but also funny in his gloomy, Eeyore-like pessimism.[18] In *The Magician's Nephew*, which was written next, Lewis adds plenty of comedy kids can appreciate, especially in the figure of Uncle Andrew. In this book, he even includes the origins of Narnian humor, when Aslan explains to the Jackdaw, "Little friend ... you have not *made* the first joke; you have only *been* the first joke."[19] As all the animals laugh, Aslan speaks, seeming to give voice to the insight that Lewis himself had while writing *The Voyage of the "Dawn Treader"*: "Laugh and fear not, creatures. Now that you are no longer dumb and witless, you need not always be grave. For jokes as well as justice come in with speech."[20]

Second New Direction: Satire of Modernism

A second new direction is introduced already in the *Dawn Treader*'s first paragraph, with Lewis' satirical description of the Scrubb family: "[Eustace] didn't call his father and mother Father and Mother but 'Harold' and 'Alberta.'

---

[17] *The Silver Chair*, 566, chap. 3.

[18] See, for example, Puddleglum's description of the perils of the journey ahead in ibid., 581, chap. 5.

[19] *The Magician's Nephew*, 72, chap. 10.

[20] Ibid.

They were very up-to-date and advanced people. They were vegetarians, non-smokers and teetotallers and wore a special kind of underclothes. In their house there was very little furniture and very few clothes on the beds and the windows were always open."[21] There's no passage like that in *The Lion, the Witch and the Wardrobe* or *Prince Caspian*, no previous example of social commentary, with Lewis implicitly remarking on life in contemporary England. The specific target here is "modernism." Lewis is mocking modern ideas about parenting and diet and lifestyle. Some of the satire sounds odd in the twenty-first century, especially his jab at nonsmokers, but he is mainly criticizing an early form of the "health and wellness" ideology. And as Lewis' student and friend Derek Brewer comments, "None of us in those days realised" the dangers of smoking.[22]

As the book goes on, Eustace Scrubb keeps boasting about modern "liners and motor-boats and aeroplanes and submarines."[23] He reads modern books, which have "a lot to say about exports and imports and governments and drains" but are "weak on dragons."[24] He stands in stark contrast to the world of Narnia. Lewis begins calling attention to something that was quietly in the background of the first two books, the fact that Narnia is not modern—it is medieval, with knights and swords and castles and damsels in distress. It is a pastoral paradise, unspoiled by the side effects of urbanization and industrialization. It has no cities, no factories, no stores, no pollution, and no poverty, though it does take for granted many familiar, useful things

[21] *The Voyage of the "Dawn Treader,"* 425, chap. 1.

[22] Derek Brewer, "The Tutor: A Portrait," in *C. S. Lewis at the Breakfast Table,* 56.

[23] *The Voyage of the "Dawn Treader,"* 437, chap. 2.

[24] Ibid., 464, chap. 6.

that require labor, manufacture, and trade, such as Mrs. Beaver's sewing machine.[25] (Who made it? Where did she buy it? Bought it with what?)

Starting with *The Voyage of the "Dawn Treader,"* Narnia becomes not just premodern but antimodern. Lewis claimed (whether seriously or jokingly) that he himself was antimodern, that he even took pride in it. In 1944, he received a letter from Walnut Creek, California, offering him membership in the Society for the Prevention of Progress, to which he replied: "While feeling that I was born a member of your Society, I am nevertheless honoured to receive the outward seal of membership. I shall hope by continued orthodoxy and the unremitting practice of Reaction, Obstruction, and Stagnation to give you no reason for repenting your favour."[26]

One of the reasons Lewis and Tolkien bonded so closely is that they shared a dislike of modern times and modern things. Tolkien, like Lewis, had a deeper affinity for earlier ages than for the present. Tolkien's academic specialty was languages of the Anglo-Saxon period, and part of him craved that premodern culture over the one of his day, marked by what he called the evil spirit of "mechanism, 'scientific' materialism, [and] Socialism."[27] Tolkien felt deeply "the heart-racking sense of the vanished past."[28] He liked "unmechanized farmlands" and "good plain food (unrefrigerated)."[29] "How I wish," he wrote in 1944, that "the 'infernal combustion' engine had never

[25] See *The Lion, the Witch and the Wardrobe,* 142–43, chap. 7.

[26] *The Collected Letters of C. S. Lewis,* ed. Walter Hooper (New York: HarperCollins, 2004–2007), 2:613–14.

[27] *The Letters of J. R. R. Tolkien,* ed. Humphrey Carpenter (Boston: Houghton Mifflin Company, 1981), 110.

[28] Ibid.

[29] Ibid., 288–89.

been invented."[30] Middle Earth is premodern. Travel is done by horse, foot, or boat; lighting comes from candles and torches; battles are fought with swords, spears, arrows, and catapults. In a letter, Tolkien says, "Imaginatively this 'history' is supposed to take place in a period of the actual Old West of this planet."[31]

In creating the character of Eustace, Lewis brings the modern world into Narnia in order to comment on social issues that he was concerned about in the 1950s. This is new, different from *The Lion, the Witch and the Wardrobe* and *Prince Caspian*. The closest to contemporary social issues either of those books gets is this sentence in *Prince Caspian*: "[Caspian] began to see that Narnia was an unhappy country. The Taxes were high and the laws were stern."[32] Neither *The Lion, the Witch and the Wardrobe* nor *Prince Caspian* has a sentence like Eustace's reply when Edmund and Lucy address Caspian as their King. In his notebook, Eustace writes, "I said I was a Republican [not a monarchist]; but [Caspian] had to ask me what that meant! He doesn't seem to know anything at all."[33]

This attention to political and economic issues leads to the humorous and satirical scene where Governor Gumpas is deposed by Caspian and Lord Bern in the fourth chapter of *The Voyage of the "Dawn Treader."* Lewis clearly is satirizing modern bureaucrats with their desks full of letters, dossiers, ink pots, pens, sealing wax, and documents, and their personal inaccessibility: "No interviews ... except between nine and ten p.m. on second Saturdays."[34] When Caspian points out that slavery is contrary to the ancient

[30] Ibid., 77.
[31] Ibid., 220.
[32] *Prince Caspian*, 341, chap. 5.
[33] *The Voyage of the "Dawn Treader,"* 437, chap. 2.
[34] Ibid., 449, chap. 4.

custom and usage of Narnia, Gumpas replies, "Necessary, unavoidable,... an essential part of the economic development of the islands."[35] But the slave trade is hardly a sound economic development; there is no production or import of real goods that enhance the quality of individual or community life—it involves only paper profits resulting from the dehumanization of other individuals. Thus Caspian replies, exposing the practice for what it is, "I do not see that [the slave trade] brings into the islands meat or bread or beer or wine or timber or cabbages or books or instruments of music or horses or armour or anything else worth having. But whether it does or not, it must be stopped." And Gumpas replies in what Lewis would regard as modernistic thinking: "But that would be putting the clock back.... Have you no idea of progress, of development?"[36]

Lewis' word "progress" here is loaded with irony. In *Mere Christianity*, Lewis says, "You *can* put a clock back.... We all want progress. But progress means getting nearer to the place you want to be. And if you have taken a wrong turning [as Gumpas has], then to go forward does not get you any nearer."[37] In his essay "Is Progress Possible?," Lewis says, "Progress, for me, means increasing goodness and happiness of individual lives,"[38] and Lewis did not see goodness and happiness increasing in the modern world. He sums up the theme in *The Voyage of the "Dawn Treader"* by contrasting Lord Bern's estates, which Lewis describes as "happy and prosperous," with Governor Gumpas' preoccupation with "accounts and forms and rules and regulations."[39]

[35] Ibid., 450, chap. 4.

[36] Ibid.

[37] *Mere Christianity* (San Francisco: HarperOne, 2009), pt. I, chap. 5.

[38] "Is Progress Possible?," in *The Collected Works of C. S. Lewis* (New York: Inspiration, 1996), 512.

[39] *The Voyage of the "Dawn Treader,"* 447–48, chap. 4.

Similar allusions to modern social issues appear in each of the later books. In *The Horse and His Boy*, there is the unappealing description of the Calormene city Tashbaan: "What you would chiefly have noticed if you had been there was the smells, which came from unwashed people, unwashed dogs, scent, garlic, onions, and the piles of refuse which lay everywhere."[40] Lewis was not fond of London, or any other city, and it's noteworthy that there are no cities in Narnia.

In *The Silver Chair*, we learn that Eustace attends a modern school, Experiment House, one that has no spanking or other corporal punishment and seems to encourage grade grubbing, with a modern headmistress who treats bullies as "interesting psychological cases ... and talk[s] to them for hours."[41] Edmund's school in *The Lion, the Witch and the Wardrobe* was bad, but it wasn't modern. It's the same for the schools at the end of *Prince Caspian*—bad but not modern.

In addition to the satire on modern education, there is the amusing satire on modern bureaucracies generally. After the inquiry into Experiment House, friends of the headmistress saw that she "was no use as a Head, so they made her an Inspector to interfere with other Heads. And when they found she wasn't much good even at that, they got her into Parliament where she lived happily ever after."[42] And in *The Magician's Nephew*, there is a moving passage about modern warfare and nuclear weapons, when Aslan counsels Polly: "It is not certain that some wicked one of your race will not find out a secret as evil as the Deplorable Word and use it to destroy all living things.... Let your world beware. That is the warning."[43]

[40] *The Horse and His Boy*, 238, chap. 4.
[41] *The Silver Chair*, 549, chap. 1.
[42] Ibid., 633, chap. 16.
[43] *The Magician's Nephew*, 102, chap. 15.

The most trenchant example of satire on contemporary issues in the Chronicles of Narnia comes through Shift, the ape, in *The Last Battle*. Shift bears some similarities to Napoleon, the dictator pig in George Orwell's *Animal Farm* (1945), a work that Lewis admired greatly.[44] In Narnia as on Animal Farm, "All animals are equal but some animals are more equal than others." The policies of the new regime in Narnia resemble those on the farm: everyone who can work is forced to work, pulling, carrying, digging, the way animals do in other countries, all supposedly for the common good.

Lewis was concerned about the growing movement, in his day, toward collectivism and oligarchy. He disagreed with policies of the Labor government that was voted into office in Britain after World War II; and he pointed out in 1958 that government is no longer looked upon as existing to protect our rights. Modern governments aim "to do us good or make us good—anyway, to do something to us or make us something. Hence the new name 'leaders' for those who were once 'rulers.' We are less their subjects than their wards, pupils, or domestic animals. There is nothing left of which we can say to them, 'Mind your own business.' Our whole lives *are* their business."[45]

The addition of humor and satire and social commentary are significant changes in *The Voyage of the "Dawn Treader."* They enrich the reading experience, making it more entertaining and educational. Lewis and Tolkien believed that stories like theirs were meant for both children and adults (for everyone who enjoys fantasy), and these additions spoke to both audiences.

---

[44] "The Farm is a work of genius." C.S. Lewis, *On Stories and Other Essays on Literature*, ed. Walter Hooper (New York: Harcourt, Brace, Jovanovich, 1982), 101.

[45] "Is Progress Possible?," 514.

Third New Direction: Myth

The third new direction that I will discuss is Lewis' handling of myth. This one is different from the others in that it is not an addition of something that wasn't there before. Rather, this element involves improvement in what Lewis wanted all along: to write fairy stories that rise to the level of myth. I believe he does not succeed fully in the first two chronicles, but he does succeed in the last five, and his success deepens as the series progresses.

Tolkien and Lewis classified *The Hobbit* and *The Lord of the Rings* and the Chronicles of Narnia as "fairy-stories," although nowadays publishers and bookstores classify them as "fantasy." A fantasy, in literary terms, is a work that takes place in a world that exists only in the imagination of its creator and its readers. A fairy story is a fantasy that takes place in Fairyland, the realm in which fairies have their being, a realm that also contains such creatures as dwarfs, trolls, giants, witches, dragons, and elves. A good fantasy world is independent of our world and self-sufficient; all the information needed to understand actions and meanings must be available within that world. As an imaginary world, it may have natural laws different from those of our world, but once those laws are established, they must be adhered to; if they are ignored or violated, the magic spell of the story will be broken.

When fairy stories (fantasies) are especially artistic, beautiful, and moving, when they are perfect in self-contained significance, Lewis and Tolkien believe they can rise to the level of myth. They do not mean "myth" in its common, everyday use: a widely held but false belief. In literary studies, "myth" refers to stories that deal with matters beyond everyday life, things too large or deep or mysterious or incomprehensible for the human intellect to grasp, things whose significance can be dealt with only through imaginative stories. Lewis says that myths touch us deeply, in our hearts and souls, and they "shock" us "more fully awake than we are for most of our lives."[46] That was the kind of story Lewis tried to write in *The Lion, the Witch and the Wardrobe*.

But from the first there has been a confusion or disagreement about the form of the Chronicles of Narnia. Some readers and critics have read the books as "allegories," works whose events and characters "stand for" or point to things outside their fantasy world. An early review said that "the allegory, for an adult at least, is clear." Similarly, Charles A. Brady wrote, "Allegory is strong in Narnia,"[47] and John W. Montgomery held that "the Narnia Chronicles contain powerful and deep Christian allegory woven into their very fiber."[48] Ironically, all of these critics praise Lewis for succeeding in what he was not intending or attempting to do. Lewis and Tolkien both insisted that their works were not allegories. Tolkien wrote in the foreword to *The Lord of the Rings*, "I cordially dislike allegory in all of its manifestations," and he disliked it because he, like Lewis, did not intend or want objects, characters, and actions to have one-to-one connections with things or meanings outside the story.

Lewis tried to set matters straight in his essay "Sometimes Fairy Stories May Say Best What's to Be Said": "Some people seem to think that I began by asking myself how I could say something about Christianity to children; then fixed on the fairy tale as an instrument; then ... drew up a

[46] *George MacDonald: An Anthology*, ed. C.S. Lewis (San Francisco: Harper-Collins, 2001), xxxii.

[47] Charles A. Brady, "Finding God in Narnia," *America*, October 27, 1956.

[48] J.W. Montgomery, "The Chronicles of Narnia and the Adolescent Reader," *Journal of Religious Education* 54, no. 5 (1959): 418–28.

list of basic Christian truths and hammered out 'allegories' to embody them. This is all pure moonshine. I couldn't write in that way at all."[49] In contrast, a "good myth," Lewis wrote, is "a story out of which ever-varying meanings will grow for different readers and in different ages." Such a myth "is a higher thing than allegory (into which one meaning has been put). Into an allegory a man can put only what he already knows: in a myth he puts what he does not yet know and [could] not come to know in any other way."[50] To Lewis and Tolkien, myth transcends allegory because the greater imaginativeness of myth can enable an author to achieve more and better results than he or she could have planned or intended.

As Lewis worked on *The Lion, the Witch and the Wardrobe*, his aim was to create myth, and the climax of the story draws upon one of the great, universal myths, the archetypal nature myth of "the dying and reviving god." Lewis said of this myth in its pagan form that he had responded to it the way one should respond to myth. In a letter to his friend Arthur Greeves, Lewis wrote, "I was prepared to feel the myth as profound and suggestive of meanings beyond my grasp even tho' I could not say in cold prose 'what it meant.'"[51] This myth had been instrumental in his conversion to Christianity, as a conversation he had with Tolkien and Hugo Dyson convinced him that "the story of Christ is simply a true myth: a myth working on us in the same way as the others, but with this tremendous difference that *it really happened.* . . . It is God's myth where the others are men's myths."[52]

---

[49] "Sometimes Fairy Stories May Say Best What's to Be Said," in *Of Other Worlds: Essays and Stories* (New York: Harcourt, 1994), 36.

[50] *Collected Letters of Lewis*, 3:789–90.

[51] *They Stand Together: The Letters of C. S Lewis to Arthur Greeves*, ed. Walter Hooper (London: Collins, 1979), 427.

[52] Ibid., 431.

With this great myth at the center of *The Lion, the Witch and the Wardrobe*, why did readers and critics, including Tolkien, respond to the book as allegory instead of recognizing it as myth? The answer, I think, is that Lewis unintentionally invites us to read it allegorically by making the context of Aslan's death and resurrection almost totally biblical and Christian. He didn't bring out the universality of the myth by including allusions or details from the Greek or Germanic nature myths that he loved. Instead, the details allude to or echo the Bible, which makes it seem like Lewis wants readers to look for allegorical parallels between Aslan and Jesus. If you've read the book, you're probably familiar with examples. The scene of Aslan being mocked, tortured, and killed on the stone table has a "crowd of creatures kicking [Aslan], hitting him, spitting on him, jeering at him."[53] The similarity to Mark 14:65 is unmistakable: "Some began to spit on [Jesus],... and to strike him, saying to him, 'Prophesy!'" Likewise, "[Aslan] made no resistance at all" closely echoes Isaiah 53: "He was oppressed, and he was afflicted, yet he opened not his mouth" (v. 7). Even the stone table, with the moral law engraved on it, resembles the tablets of stone that Moses brought down from the mountain with the Ten Commandments written on them.

What difference does all of this make? The death of Aslan is a powerful scene, which has a deeply emotional effect and imaginative appeal. In one sense, whether it is allegory or myth is not important. No one would wish it to have been handled differently than it was. So allegory or myth—does it matter? Well, it mattered to Lewis, because if it's allegory, to him it is a lesser achievement than if it's myth.

[53] *The Lion, the Witch and the Wardrobe*, 181, chap. 14.

Tolkien in "On Fairy-Stories" argued that fantasy is more difficult to write than realistic fiction because the fantasy writer has to create the book's own world, not just copy the world we live in; thus, fantasy is a higher form of art, "indeed the most nearly pure form, and so (when achieved) the most potent (or powerful).... Few attempt such difficult tasks. But when they are attempted and in any degree accomplished, then we have a rare achievement of Art: ... story-making in its primary and most potent mode."[54] Lewis knew Tolkien's essay well. Only a year or two before he started writing *The Lion, the Witch and the Wardrobe*, he edited the essay for the book *Essays Presented to Charles Williams*, published in 1947. It seems possible that one effect of editing the essay was to whet his appetite for attempting that "difficult task," that most "nearly pure" form of art. And Lewis would be aware that since many readers and critics took it as allegory, not myth, he had not accomplished that rare achievement in either *The Lion, the Witch and the Wardrobe* or *Prince Caspian*. Perhaps that prodded him to try one more time—to try a different approach and make his third book less allegorical and more mythical.

Mythical characteristics are readily apparent in *The Voyage of the "Dawn Treader,"* both in the book as a whole and in key episodes of the book. Lewis draws on a range of mythlore and folklore, Christian and non-Christian. The story as a whole is a series of literal and figurative adventures that explore simultaneously the unknown Eastern Seas and a range of social, moral, and religious concerns. Running through the episodic adventures, unifying them and creating a numinous aura, is the theme of "voyaging."

[54] J. R. R. Tolkien, "On Fairy-Stories," in *Tree and Leaf* (London: Harper-Collins, 2001).

The voyage imagery gives the story the literal flavor of the sea (they "tasted the salt on their lips"[55]) and the figurative flavor of mystery and excitement that large bodies of water have always engendered. The nature of the story, and the quality of the readers' response to it, would be very different if it were a journey by land, or only a metaphorical journey. Through form, plot, setting, images, and symbols, Lewis enables readers to engage imaginatively, not just to seek intellectual meaning.

The story of Eustace in *The Voyage of the "Dawn Treader"* is a reworking of the story of Edmund in *The Lion, the Witch and the Wardrobe*. Both boys needed to receive and accept a new kind of life. But Eustace's story uses the language and techniques of imagination and myth instead of the language of allegory with its need for interpretation. From the first, Eustace is disagreeable ("Deep down inside he liked bossing and bullying."[56]) and self-centered ("Lucy gives me a little of her water ration. She says girls don't get as thirsty as boys. I had often thought this but it ought to be more generally known at sea."[57]). Eustace—in a detailed and realistic scene, through his selfishness, laziness, and greed—discovers that he has turned into a dragon, and he realizes that all along he has been selfish and obnoxious and, like Edmund, needs to go back and start over.[58]

Aslan appears, mysteriously—Eustace doesn't know if the Lion is real or a dream, or if the Lion actually speaks, though he is certain that the Lion somehow tells him to follow and that he himself is full of fear, and of awe. The Lion leads him to a pool in a garden on a mountain. The water in the pool, Eustace later tells Edmund, "was as clear as anything

[55] *The Voyage of the "Dawn Treader,"* 437, chap. 2.

[56] Ibid., 425, chap. 1.

[57] Ibid., 458, chap. 5.

[58] Ibid., 466–67, chap. 6.

and I thought if I could get in there and bathe it would ease the pain in my leg. But the lion told me I must undress first."[59] Three times Eustace peels off his dragon skin and three times it grows right back.

> Then the lion said—but I don't know if it spoke—"You will have to let me undress you." I was afraid of his claws, I can tell you, but I was pretty nearly desperate now. So I just lay flat down on my back to let him do it....
>
> Well, he pulled the beastly stuff right off—just as I thought I'd done it myself the other three times, only they hadn't hurt—and there it was lying on the grass: only ever so much thicker, and darker, and more knobbly look-ing than the others had been.... Then he caught hold of me—I didn't like that much for I was very tender under-neath now that I'd no skin on—and threw me into the water. It smarted like anything but only for a moment. After that it became perfectly delicious and as soon as I started swimming and splashing I found that all the pain had gone from my arm. And then I saw why. I'd turned into a boy again.[60]

Like *The Lion, the Witch and the Wardrobe*, this episode has Christian imagery, such as the use of the number three, the inability of Eustace to change himself, and the new clothes. But here in *Voyage of the "Dawn Treader,"* Lewis does not try to explain the imagery. Lewis just has Eus-tace tell his story and lets the story speak for itself, espe-cially through water as a Christian and universal symbol. The use of water to symbolize purification draws upon the inherent virtues of water as a cleansing agent. And the use of water (especially immersion into and rising out of

[59] Ibid., 474, chap. 7.
[60] Ibid., 474–75, chap. 7.

water) is effective in symbolizing rebirth because of the archetypal associations of water with death and life. This stage of Eustace's spiritual journey, then, which began as he fell into the briny waters of a picture at home, culminates in the well of life on a mountain in Narnia. In the words of the story, after his experience on Dragon Island, Eustace "began to be a different boy."[61] He had been on the wrong road, he did an "about-turn" (as Lewis put it in *Mere Christianity*) and returned to the right road, and now he is ready to move on.

A similar use of story, symbol, metaphors, and myth occurs as Lucy looks into the book in the Magician's house. It is a mysterious book. "There was," for example, "no title page or title; the spells began straight away." Also, "you couldn't turn back. The right-hand pages, the ones ahead, could be turned; the left-hand pages could not." As Lucy gazes at a page, she sees a picture of a girl dressed exactly like herself, standing at a desk reading a huge book. And "the girl in the picture was Lucy herself." What she sees in the book is "much more than a picture. It [is] alive."[62] It is a metaphor for Lucy's life. Within that book of life are a variety of opportunities to do good ("how to remember things forgotten") or evil ("how to give a man an ass's head"), and a variety of temptations, some of which hold little or no appeal for Lucy, some of which attract her and could well catch her in their "spell." It is these latter that develop her character the most. The temptations of pride and curiosity try her greatly, and she even gives in to curiosity, to her sorrow and loss.

But there is more in this scene than mere metaphors and symbols, for the Magician's book is not only a book of life with all its experiences and temptations; it is also,

[61] Ibid., 476, chap. 7.
[62] Ibid., 495–97, chap. 10.

in a deeper sense, a book of Life. Lucy encounters a series of pages that are more like a story than a spell (just as the scene here leaves allegory behind and speaks to the heart with images). In them she reads "the loveliest story [she] ever read or ever shall read in [her] whole life."[63] Mysteriously, she does not remember the story after she finishes, but she can recall a few of the images in it: "It was about a cup and a sword and a tree and a green hill."[64] These images can be taken as Christian (the cup as the chalice used by Jesus and his disciples, the sword as the spear that pierced Jesus' side, the tree as the Cross, and the green hill as Calvary), but they don't have to be Christian. The images could be *suggesting* (but no more than suggesting) that any lovely story can remind us of the beauty and lovingness of Christ. Explanations and interpretations are not needed. Explanations and interpretations are not the point, which may be why Lucy does not remember the plot of the story, but only its quality.

Lewis gives a new level to myths here. Just as myths of our world can be realities in Narnia, as Father Christmas and Bacchus are, so what is reality in our world can become myth in Narnia. If Lucy were a Narnian, reading the beautiful story in the Magician's book would not be enough: she would need to grow closer to God in his Narnian incarnation as Aslan. But Lucy isn't a Narnian. For her, knowing Aslan is not enough. She needs to grow closer to God in his earthly incarnation as Jesus. Thus Lucy asks Aslan, "Shall I ever be able to read that story again, the one I couldn't remember? Will you tell it to me, Aslan? Oh do, do, do," and Aslan replies, "Indeed, yes, I will tell it to you for years and years."[65]

[63] Ibid., 497, chap. 10.
[64] Ibid.
[65] Ibid., 499, chap. 10.

For us, as persons living in our world and reading the Narnian myths for enjoyment or for spiritual growth, the situation is reversed. The Narnian myth about Aslan's love and sacrifice can be *a* means of drawing us nearer to the divine realities in our world. But that would not be enough by itself. That is made clear by a mythic passage at the end of the voyage, when Edmund, Lucy, and Eustace arrive at the end of the world and wade to the shore. In a scene that rises to the level of high myth, although it certainly contains parallels to the Christian Gospels, the children see a lamb cooking fish on the seashore, and they ask if there is a way into Aslan's country from their own world.

> "There is a way into my country from all the worlds," said the Lamb; but as he spoke his snowy white flushed into tawny gold and his size changed and he was Aslan himself, towering above them and scattering light from his mane.
>
> "Oh, Aslan," said Lucy. "Will you tell us how to get into your country from our world?"
>
> "I shall be telling you all the time," said Aslan. "But I will not tell you how long or short the way will be; only that it lies across a river. But do not fear that, for I am the great Bridge Builder."[66]

It is a powerfully evocative passage, making valuable use of Christian images and symbols (light, lamb, lion, river, door); biblical allusions (the passage as a whole alludes to John 21:4–19, and "I AM" is the name revealed by Yahweh to Moses in Exodus 3:14); and archetypal symbolism (a river is a traditional symbol of death and a bridge is an archetypal symbol of a passage to another world). But readers are not asked to isolate such features and interpret

[66] Ibid., 540–41, chap. 16.

their individual effects separately; all components unite to let the passage appeal directly to the emotions and imagination. It contains, as Lewis said great myth always does, more than the author could have intended, and it conveys, through story and symbols, things the author could not have put into other words.

For children and adults reading the Narnian stories in our world, this episode and the other Narnian myths can be a useful part of their spiritual journey, but further progress toward spiritual maturity requires more, as Aslan explains to Lucy and Edmund when Lucy asks when they will return to Narnia.

> "Dearest," said Aslan very gently, "you and your brother will never come back to Narnia.... You are too old, children,... and you must begin to come close to your own world now."
>
> "It isn't Narnia, you know," sobbed Lucy. "It's *you*. We shan't meet *you* there. And how can we live, never meeting you?"
>
> "But you shall meet me, dear one," said Aslan.

Edmund asks if Aslan is in our world, too, and Aslan replies, "I am.... But there I have another name. You must learn to know me by that name. This was the very reason why you were brought to Narnia, that by knowing me here for a little, you may know me better there."[67] Aslan's words explain Lewis' hopes and intentions for this whole series: that readers will get to know Aslan through myths and images about him in the Chronicles of Narnia.

I believe Aslan's words at the end of *The Voyage of the "Dawn Treader"* express a realization that Lewis arrived at as he explored new directions in this book, a realization

[67] Ibid., 541, chap. 16.

that enabled him to write four more chronicles, each containing at least one powerful mythic episode or passage. In *The Silver Chair*, there is the resurrection scene after Aslan, Jill, and Eustace come upon Caspian lying dead in a stream of water; a drop of Aslan's blood awakens Caspian to new life in Aslan's country. In *The Horse and His Boy*, there is the awe-filled scene in which a large, unseen creature walks through the night alongside Shasta and answers Shasta's question "Who are you?"

> "Myself," said the Voice, very deep and low so that the earth shook: and again "Myself," loud and clear and gay: and then the third time "Myself," whispered so softly you could hardly hear it, and yet it seemed to come from all round you as if the leaves rustled with it.[68]

In *The Magician's Nephew* there is the wonderful creation myth and in *The Last Battle* the equally wonderful end-of-the-world myth and world-beyond-the-end-of-the-world myth of Aslan's country, of heaven.

The voyaging myth in *The Voyage of the "Dawn Treader"* relates especially well to the liturgical season of Lent, a season of penitence and spiritual growth for Caspian, Lucy, and Eustace. But it relates well also to one other character—perhaps (after Aslan) the most important character in the story: Reepicheep the mouse, with his giant-sized longing to follow Aslan and to be with Aslan forever. As the *Dawn Treader* nears Reepicheep's goal, the images of sea and ship return. The sea is the Silver Sea, a body of sweet water covered with lilies, a traditional symbol of life. The ship is a coracle, a small boat with room only for Reepicheep—in this final stage

---

[68] *The Horse and His Boy*, 281, chap. 11.

of his journey toward spiritual fulfillment, toward union with Aslan, he must "go on alone."[69]

The sense of "voyaging," with its peculiar overtones of romance and nostalgia, is especially enhanced at the end of the story by two images—mountains and music—that Lewis always associated with longing. As Reepicheep leaves the children to go on in his coracle and bids them goodbye, he tries to be sad for their sakes, but he quivers with happiness as he gets into the coracle and takes up the paddle. The coracle rushes up a smooth, green wave, and they see him for a moment at the top. "Then it vanished, and since that moment no one can truly claim to have seen Reepicheep the Mouse. But my belief [says the narrator] is that he came safe to Aslan's country and is alive there to this day."[70] His longing for Aslan's country and for being in Aslan's presence has been perfectly fulfilled.

May that be true for all of us as well.

---

[69] *The Voyage of the "Dawn Treader,"* 539, chap. 16.
[70] Ibid., 539–40, chap. 10.

IV

THE SILVER CHAIR

On Knowing Him Here for a Little

Part IV

Madeline Infantine

Perhaps you do not see
quite as well as you think.

Here, you are sent
on his breath, asked
to remember his signs.

Signs, not said
in the morning, not said
awake in the middle of the night.

Not said
in the thickening air, not said
when strange things come
when shadows call. Will you
know him here? Remember him?

Some forget him
on the steep crag
as the night drags
under the ruined city. We tire
of signs said, believed, remembered.

His is the wild breath, the gentle sign,
song to send sore bones home, to see
the sun, the stars, the sea, the trees
as if at first sight.

Here, you forget him, and yet—
                he knows you still, his name
                bright and real against the pale world.

Out of the Shadows: C. S. Lewis and the Idea of Education in *The Silver Chair*

Rebekah Lamb

The first story I read on my own was C. S. Lewis' *The Horse and His Boy*. Five years old and frustrated with my reading primers, I resolved to join my older sisters in their independent forays into the world of Narnia. I was initially resistant to the efforts reading involved, but I was won over to the task when I saw how the Chronicles of Narnia captivated my sisters. Since then, reading has become an abiding passion in my life, but one that I only acquired in the first instance through the desire to imitate the people I loved and admired.

Rather like René Girard, who reminded us that desire is mimetic, Lewis was convinced that our loves and interests emerge as we seek to imitate the people we care about, and that the books we read can help form our moral discernment and religious commitments.[1] Our affections do not grow in a vacuum. For Lewis, they are principally formed in childhood, under the care of our teachers, parents, and other guardian figures (for better, for worse). Bearing his

---

[1] René Girard, *The One by Whom Scandal Comes: Studies in Violence, Mimesis and Culture*, trans. Malcolm B. DeBevois (East Lansing: Michigan State University, 2014). See also C. S. Lewis, *Experiment in Criticism* (Cambridge: Cambridge University Press, 2012).

own difficult childhood in mind, however, he maintained that literature also has a special capacity to supplement (and potentially redress) the kind of formation we receive, especially in our early years.

To Lewis' mind, writers serve as a distinctive kind of educator, related to parents and teachers but also profoundly different from them—different by necessity. An author, he writes, stands "outside" the realm of the traditional educator, uniquely able to induct children into imagined worlds in which they must make decisions and assessments of their own.[2] Unlike the parent, teacher, or uncle, the author is a "freeman and an equal, like the postman, the butcher; and the dog next door."[3] The author is therefore a liminal kind of figure, within yet also beyond the bounds of the child's environment and routines. As a result, writers can help further initiate children into their independence, enabled through acts of reading, of interpretation—which, in turn, assist in emotional maturation and moral formation. That noted, Lewis also held that guides to interpretation are as important to children's experiences of literature as teachers for initiating children into the world of literacy.[4] Guidance, in fact, is at the heart of Lewis' idea of education.

In this chapter I examine Lewis' conviction that learning how to interpret what we read is a lifelong, communal enterprise, and one that contributes to our overall moral education. More specifically, I will consider the degree to which *The Silver Chair* operates, at one level, as an outworking of Lewis' philosophy of education or moral

[2] C. S. Lewis, "On Three Ways of Writing for Children," in *On Stories and Other Essays in Literature* (New York: Harcourt Brace Jovanovich, 1982), 65.
[3] Ibid.
[4] See Lewis' own collection of essays seeking to guide interpretation, *On Stories and Other Essays in Literature*.

formation, which insists that encounters with images of goodness and love can inspire the pursuit of virtue. In this way, *The Silver Chair* complements but also adds to his seminal work, *The Abolition of Man*, which focuses extensively on the subject.

As Michael Ward puts it, Lewis understood education in the broadest sense to mean "something like a moral inheritance, the legacy of humane wisdom that the older generation imparts to the younger and which the younger have a duty to hand on in due course."[5] As with Dante's Virgil or Lewis' George MacDonald,[6] readers need guides or guardian figures to help them navigate and assess the challenges of trying to distinguish truth from falsehood, reality from appearance, substance from shadows. Bearing this in mind, we will examine Lewis' assertion that authentic education involves moral formation and that it is rooted as much in metaphysical or transcendental concerns as it is in the appreciation of history and sense experience—for, as Lewis was fond of insisting, every encounter with, or interpretation of, the world has ethical and metaphysical implications.[7]

Scholars have tended to look to Lewis' extensive corpus of writings, with special reference to the Space Trilogy (1938–1945) and *The Abolition of Man* (1943), to identify key elements of his philosophy of education.[8] Lewis himself tells us that his final novel in the Space Trilogy, *That Hideous Strength*, is an equivalent to the "serious 'point'"

[5] Michael Ward, *After Humanity: A Guide to C. S. Lewis' Abolition of Man* (Los Angeles: Word on Fire Academic, 2021), 11.

[6] In *The Great Divorce*, Lewis' narrator is led through hell by the Scottish novelist and minister MacDonald.

[7] See Lewis' "Bluspels and Flalansferes: A Semantic Nightmare," in *Selected Literary Essays*, ed. Walter Hooper (Cambridge: Cambridge University Press, 1969).

[8] See Ward, *After Humanity*.

he sought to make in *The Abolition of Man*.[9] However, we are also greatly rewarded if we turn to *The Silver Chair* as a story that further unpacks his views on formation, especially on the place of literature (of reading, interpreting, and responding) in his idea of education. For, according to Lewis, in the values and aptitudes literature uniquely imparts, we are drawn out of the shadows into the light of the sun—that classical signifier of right reason in Plato's *Republic* and Christian symbol of Christ as the "light of the world" (John 8:12).[10] In what follows, I undertake an in-depth reading of the philosophy of education found in *The Silver Chair*, with an emphasis on the role that guardian figures, memory, and language play in facilitating the maturation of the imagination and growth in virtue.

C. S. Lewis and the Idea of Education

In *The Abolition of Man*, Lewis notes that the task of the educator is to "irrigate" the deserts of students' hearts. "The right defense against false sentiments [and false interpretation] is," he says, "to inculcate just sentiments, revealing the beauty of morality along the way."[11] Drawing from Augustine, Lewis writes that virtue is "*ordo amoris*, the ordinate condition of the affections in which every object is accorded the kind of degree of love which is

[9] C. S. Lewis, preface to *That Hideous Strength* (London: HarperCollins, 1945), 345. I am grateful to Michael D. Hurley for our discussion concerning the link between the Space Trilogy and *Abolition of Man*.

[10] As we will discuss later, Lewis was informed by the long Christian tradition that saw the sun as a representation of Christ (John 8:12). In revealing the Trinity, Christ illuminates and transcends our human abilities to reason, thereby offering new horizons for our imagination.

[11] *The Abolition of Man* (London: HarperCollins, 1978), 404.

appropriate to it."[12] For Lewis, objective truth is that universal language, that harmony or music of the cosmos, to which we are meant to tune our own affections as well as our capacities to "read" the world.

We learn to cultivate ordinate affections by acknowledging what Lewis calls the "doctrine of objective value, the belief that certain attitudes really are true to the kind of thing the universe is and the kind of things we are."[13] Given this, Lewis argues that the cultivation of moral affection through authentic education is an antidote to the abuses and misuses of language, speech, and interpretation characterizing the propagandist forces and impulses of the twentieth century. What we've just outlined from *The Abolition of Man* is present throughout *The Silver Chair*, especially since the question of reading properly and the nature of education or moral formation are central and abiding concerns throughout the chronicle.

First published in 1953, *The Silver Chair* is the only chronicle within the Narniad to include an English secondary school in its setting and plot. The other chronicles mention schools, but Narnian adventures typically take place during the summer holidays, or else the dramas unfold in the context of a particular historical upheaval. *The Lion, the Witch and the Wardrobe* happens during and following the London Blitz. *The Horse and His Boy* details the fraught political tensions between the kingdoms of Narnia and Calormen, occurring during the height of Narnia's Golden Age. *The Last Battle* covers the "last days" of Narnia and the end of history itself.[14] In contrast to the other chronicles, *The Silver Chair* opens and closes on the grounds of an

[12] Ibid.
[13] Ibid., 405.
[14] *The Last Battle*, 669, chap. 1.

English secondary school, "Experiment House," which is
"co-educational" or "mixed" (although not, the narrator
implies, "nearly as mixed as the minds of the people who
ran it").[15]

The first chapter of *The Silver Chair*, titled "Behind the
Gym," not only hints at the school's deficient pedagogical
philosophy but also explicitly establishes a series of associa-
tive, atmospheric parallels between Experiment House and
the Emerald Witch's totalitarian Underland—her deep
realm—where Prince Rilian is held captive, enthralled
by her propagandic enchantments. The scene opens on
a "dull autumn day," and Jill is on a "damp little path"
behind a gym. The grass is too wet to sit on, and the only
sound is water dripping off the leaves. A stone wall prevents the students of Experiment House from walking on
the "open moor"; they are kept closed in, like the Earthmen in Underland.[16]

Like the nether regions of Dante's *Inferno* and the lower
reaches of the cave of shadows and ignorance in Plato's
Republic, both Experiment House and Underland are char-
acterized by feelings of a darkness or dullness verging on
despair. The first voice the travelers hear in Underland is
"a dark, flat voice—almost, if you know what that means,
a pitch black voice." The artificial light the Earthmen use
is cold, gray, and cheerless, and even when there is vegetation, it is "flabby like mushrooms," and the food they
are given is "flat, flabby cakes of some sort which had
hardly any taste." Lewis' catalogue of infernal and banal
adjectives for both places, including "dull," "horrid,"
"damp," "nasty," "flat," "dreary," and "hopeless"[17]—brings

[15] *The Silver Chair*, 549, chap. 1.
[16] Ibid., 553, chap. 1.
[17] Ibid., 549–55, chap. 1.

to mind Dante's experience of the banality of the citizens of hell and the inscription over hell's entrance, which reads "Abandon every hope, who enter here."[18]

We soon learn in *The Silver Chair* that Experiment House and Underland are described so similarly because they are both places shaped by abuses of language and abuses of power. We will consider this at more length when we discuss the debate between the Witch of the Deep Realm and Puddleglum. However, it is helpful first to consider the degree to which Lewis saw contemporary education and even his own personal education in childhood as severely lacking. *The Silver Chair* works through the question of education in a literary mode since, to his mind, exposure to good literature is an invaluable part of authentic formation.

Lewis suffered a great deal throughout most of his childhood education. In his autobiography, he only refers to his boarding schools by pseudonyms, such as Belsen, after the Nazi concentration camp in northern Germany. He lost his mother at the age of nine and endured especially "brutal regimes" at Wynyard School in Watford, England, which he attended between 1908 and 1910. In adulthood and especially throughout his academic career, Lewis therefore had not only a philosophical but also a personal interest in questions of formation and thought a great deal about what a good education did and did not look like.

In his writings on education, Lewis particularly criticized the 1941 Norwood Report, which proposed that external examinations in English literature should be "abolished" in schools because literature is a subjective, "sensitive

---

[18] Dante Alighieri, *Inferno*, trans. Allen Mandelbaum (London: Everyman's Library, 1982), 68.

and elusive" thing.[19] The issue Lewis had with the report principally stemmed from its promotion of a pedagogical philosophy in which curricula were developed around the "personality of the child," proposing that students should have a significant role in determining what they would study at various stages of their education.[20] Lewis preferred a tradition-led curriculum, in which students were inducted into what Matthew Arnold so famously called the long tradition of "the best which has been thought and said in the world."[21]

Counteracting the Norwood Report, Lewis wrote that there are two "types of education": a "Parthenon education" and an "optative education." The optative mood, in ancient Greek grammar, is one of the most difficult to master. It is used to express, among other meanings, wishes and hopes, and it is absent in modern Greek. Lewis notes that a great deal of work goes into being able to read the optative, but whether it is of current "use" when traveling to modern-day Greece has nothing to do with its inestimable value. He describes what he calls an optative education, which "begins," he says, "with hard, dry things like grammar, and dates, and prosody; and [so] it has at least the chance of ending in a real appreciation which is equally hard and firm though not equally dry."[22]

---

[19] Cyril Norwood et al., *Curriculum and Examinations in Secondary Schools: Report of the Committee of the Secondary School Examinations Council* (London: His Majesty's Stationary Office, 1943), 60, http://www.educationengland.org.uk /documents/norwood/norwood1943.html.

[20] Ibid., 61.

[21] Matthew Arnold, preface to *Culture and Anarchy: An Essay in Political and Social Criticism* (London: Smith, Elder, 1869), viii. Although Lewis could agree with Arnold on the value of tradition, comparisons between the two critics ends here. Among other things, their views on the nature and value of poetry were markedly different, to say the least.

[22] *On Stories and Other Essays in Literature*, 171. I am grateful to T. J. Lang for introducing me to this essay of Lewis' in the first instance.

By contrast, a Parthenon education is one in which students are taught, from the outset, merely to like or dislike the literature assigned—without having first learned what it means and what kinds of efforts are required to read it properly. With his characteristic incisiveness, Lewis sums up the Parthenon education as that which begins in "appreciation" and ends in "gush," as that which teaches a "false reverence for the Muses" by divorcing taste from discernment and, consequently, encouraging students to give lip service but not mind service to their studies.[23] The Parthenon type of education was, for Lewis, the kind promoted by the Norwood Report. He argued that an education principally rooted in students' interests fails to initiate them into a cultured practice of reading, interpretation, and appreciation; instead, it "teaches" them to "feel vaguely cultured" while actually "remain[ing]" profoundly ignorant of the price that must be paid to gain an appreciation of culture and tradition.[24] "It makes [the student] think he is enjoying poems he can't construe. It qualifies him to review books he does not understand and to be intellectual without intellect. It plays havoc, Lewis concludes, "with the very distinction between truth and error."[25] In a Parthenon education, the students' critical and emotional maturation are neither honed nor developed. Instead, the students are encouraged to express themselves as they are, with no view to personal growth.

Reading the Signs: *The Silver Chair* and an Optative Education

In *The Silver Chair*, we find Lewis far more extensively and subtly critiquing the Norwood Report and a Parthenon

[23] Ibid., 172.
[24] Ibid.
[25] Ibid.

education by placing Jill and Eustace in an experimental secondary school that operates according to an exaggerated Norwoodian philosophy. It is only through the guardianship of Aslan and other mentors, especially Puddleglum, that Jill and Eustace will graduate from a Parthenon education into an optative one. In the opening pages of *The Silver Chair*, Lewis does not outline the specifics of the curriculum at Experiment House. Instead, he focuses on its fruits. He depicts the school's atmosphere as distinctly Norwoodian and Underlandian. Following the philosophy of the "student-centric" education espoused by the Norwood Report, Experiment House believes that "boys and girls should be allowed to do what they liked" in order to be their authentic and best selves.[26] This laxity on the part of the principal and teachers has not generated a creative, aesthetic culture of appreciation but, instead, a power struggle in which "might equals right." As importantly, there is no sense of justice in the school, as selective bullying goes unpunished; in fact, bullying constitutes the social fabric of the school. The bullies, known as the collective "they," consistently harass Jill Pole and Eustace Scrubb—the heroes of the story who find in Narnia and their quest to save Prince Rilian the strength to mature and, by the end of the story, redress the social wrongs of Experiment House.

The absence of an optative education is felt on every page of the first chapter of *The Silver Chair*. For instance, in the very first paragraph of the story, we learn that "all sorts of things, horrid things, went on which at an ordinary school would have been found out and stopped in half a term.... [Instead] the Head said they were interesting psychological cases and sent for them and talked to

[26] *The Silver Chair*, 549, chap. 1.

them for hours. And if you knew the right sort of things to say to the Head, the main result was that you became rather a favourite than otherwise."[27] This passage tells us much of what we need to know about Experiment House and clearly calls to mind the kind of soft totalitarian atmosphere of Huxley's *Brave New World* or Orwell's *Animal Farm* (which Lewis admired), where groupthink and pseudopsychology replace any sense of morality—which is, as Lewis notes, primarily about acts and the choices related to them, not the feelings from which they arise.[28]

The same soft totalitarian focus on feeling is echoed in Underland, voiced especially by Prince Rilian while he is still under the Witch's enchantment. He impresses Jill more as selfish than as evil. When Eustace suggests that it is unjust to conquer Narnia, which is not at war with or even aware of Underland, Rilian responds, "I had never thought of it so before," but his troubled look almost immediately gives way to laughter: "But fie on gravity! Is it not the most comical and ridiculous thing in the world to think of them all going about their business and never dreaming that under their peaceful fields and floors, only a fathom down, there is a great army ready to break out upon them like a fountain!"[29] The consideration of immense and objective moral evil immediately yields to his subjective emotional response to it.

In exclusively privileging feeling and unchecked desire, Experiment House also suspends the ethical. This helps us understand why Aslan arranges a moral reckoning for the school at the end of the story. But the end of the story is not the first time Aslan attends to the problems

[27] Ibid.
[28] See *Mere Christianity* (London: HarperCollins, 1980), 5–8.
[29] *The Silver Chair*, chap. 11.

of Experiment House. At one level, his calling of Jill and
Eustace into Narnia to seek out Prince Rilian is part of his
plan to provide them with a better education, an authentic moral formation. As the ultimate guardian figure,
Aslan plays the role of teacher and educator throughout
The Silver Chair, assigning to Jill and Eustace the difficult
yet fulfilling experience of an optative education. Specifically, he teaches Jill, Eustace, and Puddleglum what
authentic dedication to values involves and requires.
There are already hints of Aslan's role as educator in the
opening pages of *The Silver Chair* when we learn that Eustace's previous trip to Narnia, detailed in *The Voyage of the
"Dawn Treader,"* had morally transformed him. Jill con-
firms that he used to be a "little tick" but is now a rather
decent person.[30]

Although Aslan is the transformative guide, Puddleglum, with all his obvious faults, also serves as a mentor.
This unlikely mentorship begins when, to the children's
great relief, he takes it upon himself not just to direct them
on their quest but to accompany them. They will not be
left to wander alone in a strange land like victims of a
Parthenon education, who are expected to interpret and
assess literature without first understanding or appreciating
it. There may be another echo of Lewis' criticism of the
Norwood Report, which skips over the actual experience
of the literature to arrive at its critique, in Puddleglum's
response to Jill when she tells him eagerly, "We've got to
start by finding a ruined city of giants." He says ("drily," in
humorous contrast to his ever damp surroundings), "Got
to start by *finding* it, have we?... Not allowed to start by
looking for it, I suppose?"[31]

[30] Ibid., 550, chap. 1.
[31] Ibid., 582, chap. 5.

Aslan's Signs and the Nature of Authentic Education

In *The Silver Chair*, Aslan's main role as educator is primarily revealed through his interactions with Jill, as seen in the early chapters of the chronicle. Jill encounters Aslan for the first time on his mountain, the "Mountain of Aslan," which is located "high above and beyond the end of the world in which Narnia lies."[32] The mountain is a composite of a series of holy places representing both revelation and instruction in holy things. The mountain is the place from which Aslan first teaches Jill about her quest and the signs she will need to follow and interpret to be successful in completing it. Jill is tasked with bringing Aslan's vision of a restored Narnian kingdom to fruition. However, in giving Jill the four signs as guidelines for her quest, Aslan is also offering her a path toward a richer view of reality, toward a deeper (albeit gradual) understanding of herself and the purposes of language. To adapt a phrase of Seamus Heaney, Aslan's assignment of the signs to Jill "extends" her alphabet—offering her new things to think, hope, and say about existence and the world around her.[33]

We especially see this from the outset of chapter 2 when, by virtue of his very presence, Aslan imparts to Jill a greater sense of the sacred and her dependence as a creature. In other words, Aslan awakens in Jill a greater awareness of the numinous. When Jill first meets Aslan, she is filled with existential fear and trembling. Resembling one of the "lions in Trafalgar Square," he looks straight at Jill, making it clear that he already "knew her quite well."[34]

[32] Ibid., 560, chap. 2.
[33] Seamus Heaney, *The Redress of Poetry* (London: Faber and Faber, 1995), 17.
[34] *The Silver Chair*, 557, chap. 2.

A stare-off ensues. Jill fears moving away from the Lion too quickly, and he gives her no reassurance in their initial conversations that he means her no harm. When he first addresses her, Aslan's words are rich in biblical resonances as he invites her to come closer to him: "If you're thirsty, come and drink," he says, as he knows she's tired, lost, and in need of water.[35] Although his invitation terrifies her, Jill is also filled with awe and experiences all the affective marks of a prophet before the strange and terrifying other-ness of the divine.

Aslan's voice changes Jill. Before he speaks, Jill is afraid that she might be killed; after he speaks, she is filled with a sense of holy fear, an awe before the splendor of beauty. Throughout the Chronicles of Narnia, various characters feel similar kinds of awe. When Aslan sings forth the Nar-nian cosmos, Diggory is reported to feel that the Lion's voice is too awesome, too beautiful to bear.[36] When the beavers recite the prophecy of Aslan's return to Narnia, each Pevensie child feels a different kind of fear—ranging from awe and reverence to joy or disgust, depending on their spiritual dispositions.[37] In Jill's case, the voice of Aslan inspires in her both awe and, surprisingly, trust; she wants to drink from the stream after she hears him invite her. "Her mind suddenly made itself up," and she dares to enter into conversation with the majestic Lion.[38]

---

[35] Ibid.

[36] See *The Magician's Nephew*, chap. 9.

[37] See *The Lion, the Witch and the Wardrobe*, chap. 7.

[38] *The Silver Chair*, 558, chap. 2. Lewis is adapting the notion of the numinous as presented by Rudolf Otto, who remarks that "deeply-felt religious experi-ence, as little as possible qualified by other forms of consciousness," engenders in the person a desire to proclaim a "self-confessed feeling of dependence" and a sincere admission that he or she is "but dust and ashes." This feeling of utter dependence in the face of the divine induces "creature-consciousness or creature-feeling," "the emotion of a creature, abased and overwhelmed by

Before Aslan gives Jill her quest, he requires that she undergo an examination of conscience; she is encouraged to confess the sin she committed before she was barely two minutes in Narnia. When Jill and Eustace first land on Aslan's mountain, Jill shows off by standing too close to the cliff's edge so as to look out on the land. Worried she will fall, Eustace tries to pull her back and, in so doing, falls off the precipice himself, leaving Jill alone on the mountain and sobbing over what she has done. Aslan encourages in Jill the bravery to own up to the pride that led to Eustace's fall, and she does this quite readily, without any of the equivocation or excuses she and Eustace will later try to employ when seeking material comfort in Harfang Castle (at the expense of their mission). Aslan praises Jill's honest confession, telling her she gave a "very good answer" in so willingly owning her guilt and expressing contrition.[39] Having received her confession, Aslan then entrusts to Jill the four signs that will guide her in the quest that she, Eustace, and, eventually, Puddleglum must undertake to save Prince Rilian.

Attentive to the medieval, exegetical tradition (which employed a fourfold method of interpretation), Lewis draws our attention to the moral and spiritual dimensions inherent in Aslan's signs. It is worth reviewing the content of the signs so we can think through the ways in which they signify. They are outlined by Aslan in sequential order, organized around a series of personal encounters:

its own nothingness" in the face of that "which is supreme above all creatures." This creature-consciousness manifests itself in "the hushed, trembling, and speechless humility of the creature in the presence of ... that which is a Mystery inexpressible and above all creatures." Having been now awakened to her "creature-consciousness," Jill is now receptive to the words of Aslan. See Rudolf Otto, *The Idea of the Holy*, trans. John W. Harvey (Oxford: Oxford University Press, 1958), 8, 10, 13.

[39] *The Silver Chair*, 558, chap. 2.

[When] Eustace sets foot in Narnia, he will meet an old
and dear friend. He must greet that friend at once.... Second: you must journey out of Narnia ... till you come to
the ruined city of the ancient giants. Third: you shall find
a writing on a stone in that ruined city, and you must do
what the writing tells you. Fourth: you will know the lost
prince ... by this, that he will be the first person you have
met in your travels who will ask you to do something in
... the name of Aslan.[40]

Each of these signs carries within it symbolic, moral, and
social significances, relating to personal relationships, the
importance of Narnian history, and the invaluable links
between the self, others, and the social order.

In seeking out Prince Rilian, Jill and Eustace will need
to read the people and environments around them carefully, attending to the history of the Narnian people and
Narnian civilization. Most importantly, their quest requires
them to learn, reverence, and trust the sacred name of
Aslan. The four signs are therefore not only a series of tasks
to complete or an exam to pass. They also assist Jill in
her optative education, teaching her how to find new and
deeper ways of seeing and interpreting existence.

Importantly, Aslan tells Jill that seeing and then reading or interpreting these signs will be difficult in Narnia,
even at the literal level. This is why Aslan first prompts Jill
to make a spiritual self-examination before giving her the
signs; self-knowledge is required in order to find and follow the truth. Moreover, Aslan charges Jill to remember
the signs by repeating them to herself every day, reciting
them according to the rhythmic patterns associated with
daily prayers and devotions. Echoing the divine injunc-
tion found within the Shema (Deut 6:4–9), Aslan tells

[40] Ibid., 559, chap. 2.

Jill to ponder on his words day and night. "Remember, remember the signs," he tells her. "Say them to yourself when you wake in the morning and when you lie down at night, and when you wake in the middle of the night. And whatever strange thing may happen to you, let nothing turn your mind from following the signs."[41] He also warns her that it is easier to remember these signs atop the mountain where the "air is clear" than it shall be down in Narnia where the air "thickens."[42] Here, in emphasizing the role of memory, Aslan is following the Augustinian and medieval understanding that knowledge is acquired through recollection, by remembering the reality we have forgotten through our fallenness (which engendered our state of confusion and ignorance in the first place).

One of Lewis' major concerns with the Norwoodian philosophy of education was its lack of interest in the cultivation of memory, that faculty of the mind which, for the medieval and classical philosophers, is essential for the retaining and consideration of knowledge in any meaningful way. (Neuroscience and psychology today tell us the same thing: the cultivation of memory has profound effects on our abilities to think critically and creatively.)[43] The profound importance of memory crops up continually throughout *The Silver Chair* and, as we will soon discuss, serves as a significant theme toward the end of the story in particular.

In addition to imparting a mode and method of learning to Jill, Aslan's teachings on the mountain also reveal things to her about his own divine nature. The signs serve

[41] Ibid., 560, chap. 2.
[42] Ibid.
[43] See, for example, Scott D. Slotnick, *Cognitive Neuroscience of Memory* (Cambridge: Cambridge University Press, 2017), or Paige E. Hochschild, *Memory in Augustine's Theological Anthropology* (Oxford: Oxford University Press, 2012).

as hints of his providential care, his concern for Narnian history, and his desire to root Jill, Eustace, and Puddle-glum in the most important things. The signs themselves, as words spoken by Aslan, serve as reflections of his nature, showing that, as Bernadette Waterman Ward puts it, the divine "acts and inheres" in his creation, caring for his creatures but speaking in veiled, poetic ways so as to respect their intelligence and free response.[44] Lewis' sense of the signs and how they function arises, in part, from his deep appreciation of Scripture, particularly the theology of the Gospel of John in which the signs Christ works are indicative of, and witnesses to, the kind of God who is performing them. Of course, Lewis' idea of the nature and function of signs also grows from his devoted reading of George MacDonald, the author who Lewis says first imparted to him the "quality" of "holiness."[45]

In his 1867 essay "The Imagination, Its Function and Its Culture," MacDonald dwells on the nature of signs in the created world, arguing that they invite us to be careful readers of the truth God communicates about himself in, with, and through the world he made. The world, Mac-Donald says, is "an inexhaustible wardrobe for the cloth-ing of human thought," but it also reminds us that we are not supposed to think about ourselves alone. Rather, we are to "watch" the world's "signs" to see "manifestations" of the Creator, and he especially appeals to the Hebrew poets and the Book of Psalms to make this point.[46]

---

[44] Bernadette Waterman Ward, *Word and World: Philosophical Theology in Gerard Manley Hopkins* (Washington, D.C.: Catholic University of America Press, 2002), 145.

[45] See *Surprised by Joy* (London: HarperCollins, 2012), 207–9.

[46] George MacDonald, "The Imagination, Its Function and Its Culture," in *A Dish of Orts* (London, 1893), 10, http://www.george-macdonald.com /etexts/the_imagination.html.

The educational values Aslan imparts through the revelation of the four signs do indeed teach Jill, Eustace, and Puddleglum how to read more deeply and discern the nature of providence. But these values also enable the discovery of the truth that will set Prince Rilian free and, in turn, save Narnia from a second bondage: the totalitarian rule of the Emerald Witch, who uses speech and sorcery to conceal rather than reveal the truth. This Lady of the Green Kirtle (who descends from the same Northern line of sorceresses as the White Witch who once ruled over Narnia) intends to replace Aslan's kingdom with her own surveillance state. She will construct this domain with her own images and order its rule to her private desires. While Aslan encourages the powers of memory and self-examination along with an outward-looking approach to the world, the Witch favors amnesia, power politics, and control over others. In *The Silver Chair*, the dull, dark kingdom of Underland, not unlike the grounds of Experiment House, represents the abuse of reason and an insatiable quest for power, self-promotion, and domination.

Language and Memory: Connections to Reality

The kingdom the Lady of the Green Kirtle plans to build is one possible way of ordering the Narnian world through the use of language, images, and power. But there are other kingdoms presented within *The Silver Chair*, and each one is morally measured by the way in which it rightly or wrongly uses language and memory. Like Underland, the kingdom of Harfang also runs on abuses of power and language. In Harfang, speech is solely appetitive, focused on appeasing the insatiable desires for consumption—as particularly evidenced by the giants' unethical consumption of Talking Beasts. This loss of connection to reality in Harfang is also seen in their sentimental reaction to the visitors. They call them "duck" and "precious poppet" and spoil them with treats—planning all the while to eat them at their autumn feast. They do not allow their emotions to guide them toward any considerations about the true nature of their guests. The abuse of language at Harfang is epitomized by the Witch's cruel play on words that has such dire effects when Jill naively repeats her message to the giants, "The Lady of the Green Kirtle salutes you by us and said you'd like to have us for your Autumn Feast."[47]

By contrast, the brightly colored Narnian court of Cair Paravel—the seat of King Caspian X—represents a poetic (as opposed to totalitarian or abusive) use of language. Examples abound, but we get a good sense of this when we learn that the great hall is a convivial place (neither the place of unchecked consumption as at Harfang nor a place of melancholic solitude and servitude as in Underland). The great hall features aspects of the medieval, courtly world, and, like the Anglo-Saxon mead hall, Cair Paravel is a peace-weaving place, shaped by *communitas*, recollections of Narnian virtue, and the retelling of grand old tales.[48] It is their brief stay in Cair Paravel, at the outset of their quest, that helps prepare Jill and Eustace for their journey into hostile territory, into places that contrast darkly with the splendor and goodness of Narnian culture.

The abuse of language, the abuse of memory, and the consequences of misreading reality are, of course, brought to their climax when Jill, Eustace, and Puddleglum accidentally end up where they are supposed to be: under the ruins of the ancient city of the giants, in the Marches of

[47] *The Silver Chair*, 569, chap. 8.
[48] Ibid., chap. 3.

Underland, in the place where travels happen without the light of the sun. This is the realm where everything will be tested. As Lewis turns to the kingdom of Underland and the totalitarian powers of the Witch, the sun carries a triple significance: it is a reminder of the illuminative wisdom of Aslan (which is carried in the hearts of Jill and her companions); it is the planet in which theologians dance in Dante's *Paradiso*; and it represents, in the Platonic sense, an example of the nature and form of goodness itself. In Underland, the sun is notably absent. In this realm, the only sources of light are sickly lampposts, powered by the Witch's sorcery. The Witch's lamps are but pale imitations of the sun and give off an eerie, green-gray color; theirs is a "dim, drowsy radiance" that is not strong enough to reach the roof of the cave; it only makes the immediate path somewhat discernible.[49] In Underland, no one can fully perceive, let alone interpret, things by the light of the Witch's lamps. These lights also give off a soft humming sound, evocative of a kind of "quiet sort of sadness," similar to the kind of soft music the Witch uses to keep Rilian and the pale Earthmen enthralled. The lights produce a soporific effect too, inducing a sluggishness which prevents clear thinking and attention to detail. They are the antithesis to the life-giving and dynamic music of Aslan when he sings the Narnian cosmos into being in *The Magician's Nephew*.

The dull, dim atmosphere of Underland is further compounded by the strange way the Earthmen, and even Prince Rilian, speak. Attempting to strike up a conversation with the mysterious, taciturn warden of the Marches, Puddleglum repeatedly finds that the Earthman is, frustratingly, a "chap of *one* idea."[50] Forcing the Earthmen to follow

[49] Ibid., 615, chap. 10.
[50] Ibid., 617, chap. 10.

her orders, the Witch controls and limits their memory, thereby impoverishing their speech and rendering them automatons—workmen bent on fulfilling her plans for Narnian domination. She only uses language for the purpose of directions, orders, and ceaseless work, attempting to strip communication of its poetic qualities. Rilian, in his enchanted state, similarly insists that because "under me" originally had a literal meaning (from an inscription on the grave of an ancient king), it can't also serve as a sign from Aslan about where to find the lost prince. Under the Witch's spell, he loses the ability to see layers of meaning in language. As Lewis notes in his essay, "The Death of Words," language has to be thoughtfully preserved and attended to because it is one of the first things ideologues co-opt because they know that people "do not long continue to think what they have forgotten to say."[51] In exercising mind control, the Witch seeks to remake the Underlanders in her own image and reduce language to structures of power.

Likewise, in controlling Prince Rilian, the Witch attempts to rewrite his personal history according to what suits her own desires, playing with language in the same way that Big Brother's creators manipulate public policy and communication in Orwell's *1984*. She accomplishes her enchantment by attacking the memory, that faculty of the mind which Aslan particularly cherishes. As Rilian himself admits to Jill, Eustace, and Puddleglum, he can "remember no time when [he] was not dwelling as now," at the court of his Green Lady.[52] It is only while bound to the silver chair that Rilian remembers the Green Lady is his captor, not his savior.

---

[51] *On Stories and Other Essays on Literature*, 169.
[52] *The Silver Chair*, 621, chap. 11.

It is also while bound to the silver chair that Rilian recovers his memory and Narnian identity; his sense of purpose is therefore briefly restored to him, and his facility with language becomes far more expansive and poetic. (Most tellingly of all, it is no longer self-absorbed.) Jill, Eustace, and Puddleglum are finally persuaded to believe Rilian's new facility with language points toward truth as opposed to manipulation and deceit, because the prince, pleading for his release from the silver chair, invokes the name of Aslan, thereby enacting the fourth sign. This moment in the story parallels, with only slight difference, the longing and desperation of Jill and Eustace to escape Experiment House; they also call on Aslan, asking him to bring them into the fresh and free world of Narnia. Throughout *The Silver Chair*, invoking the name of Aslan is like an act of prayer and, as such, always brings about a transformation of events and a renewal of hope—even if such renewal takes time to unfold.

In all this, we see that Aslan is the key to true reading and interpretation throughout *The Silver Chair*; he is the light that reveals itself as the source and summit of the truth. Aslan is, in a certain sense, the sun of Narnia itself; he is the source by which everything is seen in its proper context and order. In an address he gave to the Oxford Club in 1945, titled "Is Theology Poetry?," Lewis noted that we "believe that the Sun has risen" not only because we "see it"; rather, we also believe and know that the sun is risen because "by it" we "see everything else."[53] This is how Aslan works throughout Narnia. He may not always directly present himself to Narnians or to visitors from Jill and Eustace's world. But the remembrance of

[53] "Is Theology Poetry?," in *Essay Collection: Faith, Christianity, and the Church*, ed. Lesley Walmsley (London: HarperCollins, 2000), 21.

Aslan and recollections of his words and promises function as the hermeneutical key, the ideal rubric for reading reality properly. Aslan is the light by which all else in Narnia makes sense, and just as importantly, he is the source of meaning itself within the Narnian cosmos.

Throughout the chronicles and especially in *The Silver Chair*, invocations of the name of Aslan alone are enough to bring about personal and social transformation—including the "healing of harms."[54] Lewis shows this in various, pivotal moments throughout the story, but it is driven home with a special force of clarity in the dramatic debate between the Green Witch and Puddleglum, toward the novel's close. Just at the point when the Witch has nearly succeeded in re-enchanting Rilian, Puddleglum, and the children, Puddleglum musters up the courage to challenge her power by telling her about Narnia and Aslan's beauty. Attempting to resist his words, the Witch uses her soft, thrumming music to dull her prisoners' senses and cloud their memories. She nearly accomplishes her plan: as she plays her music, we learn, Jill could not stop listening to it and could no longer "remember the names of the things in our world."[55] It is clear that the magic affects everyone in the Witch's palace, but this episode suggests that the power of memory is stronger for some of the characters than for others, and it seems that the strength of this power is dependent on the degree to which each character has freely obeyed and remembered Aslan's four signs.

Jill and Eustace grow forgetful of Aslan's signs as their appetites for comfort grow during their visit to the castle of Harfang. By contrast, Puddleglum is far more reluctant

---

[54] Lewis, *The Silver Chair*, 656, chap. 16.
[55] Ibid., 630, chap. 12.

to join the children in their pleasure seeking—especially because, as he rightly reminds them, this Harfang layover is not part of Aslan's itinerary as outlined in the four signs. Indeed, throughout the story, Puddleglum is far quicker to return to the demands of their quest and face them, recalling Aslan's wishes in the process. For this reason, he bears greater immunity to the Witch's power and is better able to resist her enchantments. To Jill, Eustace, and even Rilian, resistance seems all but impossible.

Love, Desire, and Reason

From his resistance, Puddleglum summons the power to break the Witch's spell, but not through interminable debate as the Witch seeks to convince her captives that the Underland is true reality and Narnia a dream. Puddleglum's power comes directly from Aslan; it is the power of self-sacrificial, agapic love. Love is the heartbeat of Aslan's kingdom and is totally absent from the Witch's. It is the same love, the "deeper magic," that defeated the White Witch in *The Lion, the Witch and the Wardrobe*, and that also triumphs in *The Silver Chair*.[56]

Discerning that the Witch's power is rooted in deceit, Puddleglum willingly absorbs pain to feel something real. He "desperately gather[s] all his strength" and stamps out the Witch's fire, which has been powering her enthralling music, "grinding a large part of it into ashes on the flat hearth." His self-sacrifice—partly announced by the unpleasant smell of a burnt Marsh-wiggle's webbed foot—destroys the Witch's power over her prisoners. The destruction of the Witch's fire makes "everyone's brain

---

[56] See *The Lion, the Witch and the Wardrobe*, 182–86, chap. 15.

far clearer," and it is then that Puddleglum uses reasoned argument to dismantle the Witch's despair-inducing claims that Narnia does not exist.[57] He proceeds to argue that her world is a dull and impoverished one that fails to fulfil the imagination in the way that Aslan's Narnia can. He gives an argument from desire, in which he proposes that the imagination's ability to conjure up a world that surpasses Underland proves the Witch's power is ultimately impotent, unable to fulfill the longing and needs that each person possesses: "Four babies playing a game can make a play-world which licks your real world hollow," he says. "That's why I'm going to stand by the play-world. I'm on Aslan's side even if there isn't any Aslan to lead it. I'm going to live as like a Narnian as I can," he concludes, "even if there isn't any Narnia."[58] The main criticism Puddleglum levies against the Witch's Underlandian world is its failure to fulfill and transcend our deepest desires for beauty, truth, and goodness. In so arguing, Puddleglum rehearses a position Lewis often made in his own writing: we must be made for more than this fallen, limited world because we desire far more than it could ever give us. But desire is more than an argument for the truth; it is a guide to it, and one of the purposes of literature in an authentic education is to present us with transcendent objects of desire precisely for this reason. Puddleglum expresses this role of desire in education in his argument from desire: with proper moral guidance, the wishes and hopes of the optative mood can lead us to what is real and true.

While reason and philosophy have their invaluable roles to play throughout *The Silver Chair*, Aslan ultimately teaches Jill, Eustace, and Puddleglum that love is the motive power of action, meaning, and unity between

[57] *The Silver Chair*, 632, chap. 12.
[58] Ibid., 633, chap. 12.

persons. Reason follows and supports love; desire awakens and animates reason. Therefore, it is only after all three adventurers fulfill their quest (and risk their very lives in the process) that they are brought into a deeper encounter with and understanding of Aslan and his providential plans. We learn, for example, that Puddleglum's sacrifice of his foot to the Witch's fire is not only an imitation of Aslan's self-sacrificial love, evidenced by his death and resurrection in *The Lion, the Witch and the Wardrobe*; it is also a foreshadowing of the further suffering Aslan undergoes on his mountain, toward the book's close. When Jill and Eustace reunite with Aslan, he bids Eustace pierce his paw with a thick thorn, shedding drops of blood to bring King Caspian back from the dead. As Michael Ward notes, Lewis shows us throughout *The Silver Chair* that self-sacrifice and "physical risk," when committed for the sake of love and fidelity, open up the authentic path to freedom and inspire further acts of love.[59] In the chronicles, Aslan inspires characters throughout to imitate his own goodness, to love what he loves, to see and read reality as he would see and read it. In *The Silver Chair*, we see Lewis' claim that an authentic education—an optative education—is accomplished through encounters with, and personal responses to, the goodness of those we admire and, most importantly, the promptings of divine love.

Conclusion

In a letter to his friend, Malcolm Muggeridge, Lewis writes that one of the formative powers of literature is its ability to *move* us toward the good: "All that any imagery

---

[59] Michael Ward, *Planet Narnia: The Seven Heavens in the Imagination of C. S. Lewis* (New York: Oxford University Press, 2008), 136.

can do is to facilitate, or at least not to impede, man's act[s] of penitence and reception of pardon."[60] What does this mean? Several things, but of primary importance for our purposes is the understanding that pictures, images, stories, or examples of goodness can inspire in humans the pursuit of virtue. We are, after all, made in the image and likeness of God; humans are drawn to stories; we are image bearers and image makers. Part of literature's task, as Lewis saw it, is to help facilitate an ability to exercise the imagination in a way that brings us to the condition of worship of the Creator (as opposed to the worship of lesser goods or gods).

Whether a story brings us closer to truth or further away from it is one of the rubrics for assessing whether the fiction we read is formative or not. Of course, to make assessments about the value or truth-bearing capacity of literature requires that we ask (and care about) one of the most fundamental philosophical questions: "what is truth?" It is here that Lewis proposes we need the cooperation of reason and feeling, of imaginative creativity, the will, and the employment of all the mind's faculties. The question of truth is at the heart of Lewis' literary theory; it underpins his philosophy of education or formation, and it serves as a motivating principle throughout his academic and creative writing.

The Silver Chair pursues the question of truth on every page with a kind of determination and earnestness that is supported and encouraged through the characters' encounters with the wisdom that literature uniquely imparts: namely, the ability to read, interpret, remember, and love. If we recall that Lewis made the claim in *The*

---

[60] "Prayer: Letters to Malcolm," in *Selected Books* (London: HarperCollins, 1964), 286.

Abolition of Man that education is meant to be an irrigation of the desert of our hearts, an ordering of the affections in light of truth, then we can certainly interpret *The Silver Chair* as dramatizing the effects of a good education.[61] As significantly, this chronicle offers readers a vision of what life offers us if each person, sign, and situation is "given the kind of degree of love which is appropriate to it."[62]

[61] *The Abolition of Man*, 404.
[62] Ibid.

V

THE HORSE AND HIS BOY

On Knowing Him Here for a Little

Part V

Madeline Infantine

Who gives the horses newfound strength,
and sets your boat atop the stream?

Who comforts in the house of death,
when jackals prey upon your sleep?

Who moves at back of all the stories,
with breath that blows us all toward peace?

To know him here, ask him:
                    Who *are* you?

Here is the gold light,
the brightness of the grass,
and birds singing.

He is—the earth shakes with his name,
as fresh loam quakes to proclaim
the low and rumbling refrain.

He is—his name resounds, loud and bright,
as bells find song in morning light
when dawn invites the end of night.

He is—a whisper, a name hardly heard,
as rustling leaves on trees breeze-stirred
or soft-sung hymns from cooing birds.

Due North: *The Horse and His Boy*

Francesca Aran Murphy

The Horse and His Boy ranks high in the seven-tier hier-
archy of most beloved *Narnia* books. The horse's boy of
the title, Shasta, is what young people call "relatable."
We find it easy to identify with Shasta because the author
identified with him and made him sympathetic. It may be
the book in the series into which C. S. Lewis put the most
of himself.

Lewis poured much of his imaginative self-understanding
into Shasta. Shasta escapes from seemingly native servitude to an unknown land and finds that he has arrived at
his childhood home. Shasta's exile, his loss of his mother, his
travails, and his journey of self-discovery is something of
a projection of Lewis' conception of his own life. So *The
Horse and His Boy* is a philosophical adventure novel,
which dramatizes the notion of the soul as exiled from a
lost Edenic home. In many ways, this echoes C. S. Lewis'
interpretation of his life story, in *Surprised by Joy*.

"Joy" is not an everyday word in Lewis' vocabulary. It
means, for him, the experience of the deepest and most
blissful longing. Joy is not in having but in longing: its
object is all the more romantic for its anonymity, as when
the gypsy foretells that "you will meet an anonymous
stranger." Shasta finds the nameless object for which he
has unwittingly longed. So the story is about, so to say,
nameless joy, or an inborn, native desire for an unknown

and surprising home, where we will fall into the arms of our Father.

In the autobiographical *Surprised by Joy* Lewis says that when he first read the mystical fairy tales of the Scottish writer George MacDonald, he was overwhelmed with "Joy" and underwent the "baptism" of his imagination.[1] I have been told that George MacDonald claimed that people fantasize about being the long-lost children of royalty because this is what we really are. We really have a king for our Father, and our daily life here below is an exile from our true sonship of that royal Father.

In the opening pages of *The Horse and His Boy*, when we hear that the young Shasta "called him father," the reader picks up the hint that the fisherman Arsheesh is not Shasta's real father. When Shasta himself discovers this, by eavesdropping on the conversation of Arsheesh and a Calormene lord, his first thought is one of mingled relief and highfalutin fantasy: "'Why, I might be anyone!' he thought. 'I might be the son of a Tarkaan myself—or the son of the Tisroc (may he live forever)—or of a god!'"[2] It's a George MacDonald kind of thought. MacDonald himself, if my informant was correct, and certainly Lewis himself would say that the Calormene belief that their great lord and sovereign, the Tisroc (may he live forever), is descended from the god Tash is a muddled appreciation of the truth that all human beings are "children of the gods." So at the end of *The Horse and His Boy* when Shasta is recognized and welcomed with open arms by King Lune, it is a kind of return of the prodigal son, a homecoming to the authentic Father.

There is more to the autobiographical quality of the story than its illustrating a Scottish neo-Platonic theory about the

[1] See C. S. Lewis, *Surprised by Joy* (London: Fontana, 1985), 146.
[2] *The Horse and His Boy*, 208, chap. 1.

hidden immortality of the soul and its return to bliss. After Shasta discovers he is really Prince Cor, son of King Lune, he tells Aravis, his erstwhile travelling companion and fellow fugitive: "Father wants you to come and live with us. He says there's been no lady in the court ... since Mother died. Do, Aravis."[3] C. S. Lewis describes the childhood loss of his mother to cancer in *Surprised by Joy*. It is hard not to imagine that the King and Queen of Archenland are his own parents, perfected and made tolerable. King Lune is Lewis' own father, rendered likeable, and with all the sting of their incompatibility taken out.

The Horse and His Boy is the only Narnia story with no visitors from other dimensions. Queen Susan and Edmund have minor roles, but no one arrives from outside to intervene in the narrative. This makes it what the young people call "intense," meaning very focused on a single action. In his mythologized autobiography, Lewis does not want any pesky Pevensies arriving to butt in and steal the limelight. The single action of the novel is the escape of Shasta himself, Aravis, and the two horses from Calormen, the "fallen world" into the "upper world" of Archenland. The action is entirely focused in this single act of flight, much like the action of some of John Buchan's thrillers is focused on flight through English towns and Scottish moors. The *Thirty-Nine Steps* is called a "man on the run thriller," which runs from London to the North of Scotland. Lewis admired such novels. Lewis' two-horses-and-two-humans-on-the-run thriller dramatizes the return of the human soul from the far country whence it originated. It is a "wish fulfillment" in the sense that once the protagonists get to Archenland, the struggle of daily life is behind them. The two dimensions of this novel are Calormen and Narnia, and it is about escape from one to the other;

[3] Ibid., 302, chap. 14.

it would confuse the geography to introduce arrivals and interventions from any other region.

We are all careful to despise wish-fulfillment fantasy, especially one that, for example, involves marrying a mother substitute. But much of the delight of C. S. Lewis' Narnia—and the attraction of his other books—is that he puts the natural, human desire for a supernatural world into words and action. The Narnia books baptize our imagination because they express the Christian story as the fulfillment of our deepest human desire and longing. Part of the theory of all that is in Lewis' first "story book"—the nearly unreadable *Pilgrim's Regress*. From *Pilgrim's Regress* onward, for Lewis, the natural desire is a pilgrimage or a journey. I will come back to that later, but first I should remind you of the story of *The Horse and His Boy*.

The Story

The story begins in the country of Calormen, in the cottage of a fisherman named Arsheesh. Shasta toils for Arsheesh by day and night. The narrator quickly sketches a lonely and harsh childhood for Shasta. When he has a quiet moment by himself, Shasta daydreams about whatever may lie to the north of their rough demesne. As the narrator tells us:

> Shasta was not at all interested in anything that lay south of his home because he had once or twice been to the village with Arsheesh and he knew that there was nothing very interesting there.... But he was very interested in everything that lay to the North because no one ever went that way and he was never allowed to go there himself. When he was sitting out of doors mending the nets, and all alone,

he would often look eagerly to the North. One could see nothing but a grassy slope running up to a level ridge.[4]

If Arsheesh was around Shasta would ask him what lay beyond the hill. When Arsheesh was in a bad mood, he would reply by boxing Shasta's ears. If he was a bit more cheerful, Arsheesh would tell him it was a useless and impractical question. "Shasta thought that beyond the hill there must be some delightful secret which his father wished to hide from him. In reality, however, the fisherman talked like this because he didn't know what lay to the North. Neither did he care. He had a very practical mind."[5]

One night a Calormene lord, or Tarkaan, rides in. Soon he is bartering with Arsheesh for the boy: his so-called father has no qualms about selling Shasta from servitude into real slavery. The Tarkaan's horse, Bree, startles Shasta by proposing that they run away together. This is a talking Narnian horse who has been kidnapped and has spent his adult life as "a slave to humans."[6] The two fellow slaves conspire to create their own horse-powered underground railroad. They plot to flee to the North because, since he imagines that his charger is a witless, Calormene beast, the Tarkaan will conjecture they went south. Bree's desire to return home to Narnia is an added incentive.

> "O hurrah!" said Shasta. "Then we'll go North. I've been longing to go to the North all my life."
>
> "Of course you have," said the Horse. "That's because of the blood that's in you. I'm sure you're true Northern stock."[7]

[4] Ibid., 205–6, chap. 1.
[5] Ibid., 206, chap. 1.
[6] Ibid., 209, chap. 1.
[7] Ibid., 210, chap. 1.

The tale of the nocturnal escape, with Shasta's many painful falls from his perch atop Bree, is realistic. Reading it in
my boarding school at the age of ten or eleven, it never
occurred to me that it is about the journey of the soul to
God. It is much too exciting for that.

After some nights' travel, Shasta and his equine companion are terrified to find themselves being hotly pursued
by a lion. They are driven into the company of another
rider, apparently fleeing from a second lion. They gallop
knee to knee: "Indeed Bree said (afterward) that a finer
race had never been seen in Calormen."[8] After the foursome make their escape, the fine bred mare makes herself
known as a kidnapped slave from Narnia, whilst her rider
Aravis, disguised in her brother's armor, explains that she is
escaping betrothal to an elderly, hump-backed, ape-faced
Grand Vizier. The four decide that they will be less con-
spicuous if they travel together.

As the foursome approaches the capital of Calormen,
Tashbaan, they agree that if they are separated, they will
meet at the "Tombs." Like many an ancient Mediterranean
and Oriental city, Tashbaan buries its dead outside the city
walls. Like all sensible ancient people, Shasta and his companions find the Tombs terrifying. As they make their way
through the city, they are indeed separated. Shasta is mistaken for Prince Corin of Archenland and taken home by a
group of Narnian courtiers. The unintentional spy overhears
that Queen Susan has been in Tashbaan, flirting with marriage to the oldest son of the sovereign Tisroc, Prince Rabadash. She has decided to reject Prince Rabadash's hand, and
fearing that Rabadash will take her by force, the Narnian
party decide upon a nocturnal flight to Narnia in their ship.

Aravis has had her own adventures. Once recognized
by a childhood friend, she attempts to get to the Tombs

[8] Ibid., 217, chap. 2.

through the Tisroc's palace and, likewise becoming an involuntary spy, overhears Prince Rabadash's plan to win the fugitive Queen Susan by taking a party of two hundred horsemen and invading Narnia through Archenland. Once the foursome meets up again at the Tombs, they race through the desert to Archenland to warn of the oncoming invasion.

Exhausted by their trip through the desert, the four squeak through just in time to give the warning after yet another lion chases and pursues them into the mountainous pass. Shasta gives the warning, battle is raised, the Calormenes are defeated, Prince Rabadash is turned into a donkey, King Lune recognizes that Shasta is the long-lost twin brother of Prince Corin—and heir to the throne of Archenland—and all of them live happily ever after. Even the two horses, Bree and Hwin, get married, though not to one another.

Animal Companionship

Of all the Narnia books, *The Horse and His Boy* is one that perhaps most benefits from being read for the first time in childhood. A child will not see any allegory in it. What he will first delight in is the tale of animal companionship. This novel is the one in the series most focused on the Narnian animals as animals. This is an important moral concern of Lewis'. The novel was written at a time, the 1950s, when many "crossover" nonfiction stories were being published, telling tales of empathy and understanding between animals and human beings. Two of the best known books of this kind are *Born Free*, about Elsa the Lioness, and *Tarka the Otter*, about Tarka the Otter. Of course, Talking Beasts feature in all the Narnia books, but in the other chronicles, they compete much more with fauns and dragons and dwarfs as the center of attention. In *The Horse and His Boy*, the horses are the protagonists and near the moral center of the book. They are not just comedic characters: they are real horses.

On his painful journey to freedom and the North, Shasta learns to ride from Bree, and "in spite of his rude words Bree was a patient teacher. No one can teach riding so well as a horse."[9] The tale of animal-human companionship is so attractive that few children will register that Bree is a walking lesson in pride and its reward.

It is worth pointing out how appealing Lewis' talking animals are today, in our culture. Many good Christian folk think the greatest danger for humanity today is worship of the planet Earth and her ecology. And yet we can see that Lewis, with his witty, anthropomorphic animals, wrote the most appealing apologetics of the past century. Lewis' Irish love of dogs, horses, and badgers is a win for Christianity. Such affection for animals is often lost on the much poorer, more rural Mediterranean world. In Lewis' time, the traditionally Catholic rural South of Europe still saw animals in a utilitarian way, with Cartesian-Thomistic conceptions about who has a rational soul and who does not. Every year I take the Camino de Santiago; it is rare to pass an afternoon walking through the Spanish countryside without seeing dogs chained up outside farm buildings in the sun, with no water. When it comes to animals, the Anglican Lewis has got it right.

A Bit of Allegorical Moralizing

The foursome of horses and humans is not constructed simply to exhibit the delights of human-animal friendship.

[9] Ibid., 215, chap. 2.

The two pairs neatly illustrate the contrast of pride and humility. Hwin and Shasta are humble creatures, while Aravis and Bree are proud. As Lewis describes the initial relations of the four: "Hwin the mare was rather shy before a great war horse like Bree and said very little. And Aravis never spoke to Shasta at all if she could help it."[10] It is Hwin who proposes the tactic for crossing Tashbaan undetected: the horses must be muddied and cut about, and pretend to be pack animals. The charger cares all too much what others think, and strongly objects to this proposed kenosis.

> "My dear Madam," said Bree. "Have you pictured to yourself how very disagreeable it would be to arrive in Narnia in *that* condition?"
>
> "Well," said Hwin humbly (she was a very sensible horse), "the main thing is to get there."[11]

Hwin is the female counterpart of Shasta, though I hesitate to call her the heroine of the book. The character Hwin most reminds me of is Lucy Pevensie, and especially the Lucy of *Prince Caspian*. When she is weak, then she is strong. After the hot and dry trot across the desert, with Rabadash's army at their heels, it is Hwin rather than Bree who tries to insist that the horses must not rest but must increase their pace: "'P-please,' said Hwin, very shyly. 'I feel just like Bree that I *can't* go on. But when Horses have humans (with spurs and things) on their backs, aren't they often made to go on when they're feeling like this? and then they find they can. I m-mean—oughtn't we to be able to do more even, now that we're free. It's all for Narnia.'" Bree rebukes her haughtily, but as the narrator notes, Hwin was quite right. The problem for one bred

---

[10] Ibid., 225, chap. 3.
[11] Ibid., 226, chap. 3.

like Bree is that "one of the worst results of being a slave and being forced to do things is that when there is no one to force you any more you find you have almost lost the power of forcing yourself."[12]

Calormen itself, the land of kidnappees and enslavement, is constructed out of pride and self-sufficiency. Despite Bree's Narnian blood, Calormene attitudes have rubbed off on him. Bree must be doubly humbled before he can enter Narnia a free horse once again. First, he must see that it is Shasta, the mannerless, ill-bred fisherman's boy, who leaps down out of the saddle and goes back to rescue Aravis from the lion who pursues them into Archenland. He must learn before he can return to his native country to lose his "self-conceit."[13]

I'm not so keen on the second lesson that Bree learns. In the British tradition of pantomime, "pantos" are Christmas plays, usually performing tales like Cinderella, supposedly meant for children but—as my parents used to remark sarcastically—heavily laced with filthy double-entendres and coy humor that only adults find funny. The scene in which Bree is taught not to "demythologize" Aslan, King of the Beasts, seems like a Christian version of pantomime humor. For no reason connected to anything else in the book, Lewis launches into an attack on Rudolf Bultmann, John Robinson, and the then-fashionable process of "demythologizing" scriptural imagery. He has poor Bree insisting that Aslan's leonine qualities are metaphorical whilst Aslan the Lion paces on a ledge behind him. Then the Lion approaches: " 'Now, Bree,' he said, 'you poor, proud, frightened Horse, draw near. Nearer still, my son. Do not dare not to dare. Touch me. Smell me. Here

[12] Ibid., 268, chap. 9.
[13] Ibid., 275, chap. 10.

are my paws, here is my tail, these are my whiskers. I am a true Beast.' "[14] It would be very funny, especially if you have known the type of stuck-up Anglican Modernist that Lewis is satirizing. But why here? Why morph Bree the war horse into an Anglican Modernist? At a pinch one can see how refusing the real leonine physicality of Aslan reflects pride and arrogance, but this scene does not connect to anything else in the story. War horses and soldiers are not obviously given to excessively philosophical, speculative conceptions of the Scriptures. None of the Calormenes demythologize their god Tash!

The theme of pride versus humility is the moral counterpart of the overall story theme of Narnia versus Calormen, and through the four characters, we are shown that the border between good and evil runs through every heart. Even the proud Aravis, who does not care that her slave gets a whipping if she can execute her escape from marriage to the Grand Vizier, is said to be "true as steel and would never have deserted a companion whether she liked him or not."[15]

The character who is most profoundly mocked for his pride is Prince Rabadash. The penalty is imposed on him by Aslan himself: Rabadash is turned into a donkey and told that the only way to reverse the metamorphosis is to appear before the high altar of the god Tash in this donkified state. One of the advantages of C. S. Lewis over a heavier writer like J. R. R. Tolkien is that Lewis loved the whole comic tradition of English literature, from Chaucer through Austen and Dickens. Prince Rabadash is in that great tradition of stock comic buffoons. Through him Lewis manages to show that pride is fear-inspiring but also ridiculous. *The*

[14] Ibid., 299, chap. 14.
[15] Ibid., 244, chap. 6.

Horse and His Boy is a comic novel, and therefore none of its characters is utterly lost. Prince Rabadash survives his ordeal to become Rabadash the Ridiculous.

Who Are the Calormenes?

Lewis' picture of the Calormenes is colored by a dislike of "abroad," typical of an insular Englishman of his genera- tion. I once twitted my father—a Londoner—that for his generation, civilization ended at Calais. "You mean East Croydon," he answered vigorously and with feeling. Much about the Calormenes, their all-purpose southernness, could reflect anywhere in the South of Europe, from Spain, Por- tugal, to Mediterranean France and Italy. Aside from the natives, the thing that true insular Englishmen most disliked about "abroad" was the food. There was no real bread, only croissants, and the meat was mucked about with oily sauces. When George Orwell returns home to England from fighting Spanish fascists and being hunted by Spanish communists, in *Homage to Catalonia*, he cannot wait to taste food that is not cooked in oil. Cooking in butter was so obviously preferable that, down to the early 1960s, olive oil was a mark of bohemian pretentiousness. It's a great comic touch when Shasta first eats butter, amongst the Narnian Dwarfs: "It was all new and wonderful to Shasta for Calor- mene food is quite different. He didn't even know what the slices of brown stuff were, for he had never seen toast before. He didn't know what the yellow soft thing they smeared on the toast was, because in Calormen you nearly always get oil instead of butter."[16] Lewis had no taste for the Mediterranean diet. But it gets worse, of course.

[16] Ibid., 240, chap. 5.

Rivers of ink have been spilled defending and accus-
ing Lewis of making Muslims of his Calormenes. The
Calormenes *are* and must be somewhat "Arabic" or Oriental. Lewis mentions several times in *Surprised by Joy* that
he read Herodotus' histories as a schoolboy. Herodotus
describes in his history the two attempted Persian invasions
of Greece, first by Darius the Great in 490 B.C. and then,
in the Second Persian War, by Darius' son, Xerxes, in 480
B.C. The mountains of Thessaly, in northern Greece, initially held the Persians back, until Xerxes' men discovered
a narrow mountain pass, doubling back on the three hundred Spartans at Thermopylae and taking the gateway to
Greece, though they eventually lost the war. In both invasions, the Persians were ultimately repelled by the Greek
city-states, who won heroic victories at Marathon, Plataea,
and Mycale. Herodotus is an objective but not unbiased
reporter. Throughout his depiction of the Persian Wars,
he describes the Persians as slaves, fighting under the
yoke of the tyrants Darius and Xerxes, and conversely he
describes the Greeks as free men. He leaves the reader in
no doubt that these battles were fought and won, yes, by
the gods and goddesses of Greece, but also by the free
city-states—above all, the democratic city-state of Athens.
It is difficult not to think that this moral geography is the
original lever for Lewis' moral imagination, in his juxtapo-
sition of Calormen and Archenland (Thessaly) and Narnia
(Greece proper). Herodotus' histories were not in those
days esoteric knowledge. Lewis would have expected the
English schoolboys amongst his readers to know chunks of
them from their Greek Unseen textbooks.

Of course, it is anachronistic to say the Calormenes are
pre-Christian Persians and leave it at that. Englishmen of
Lewis' time were divided between the more imperialist
types, such as Rudyard Kipling, who admired India and

its Muslim population, and those like G.K. Chesterton and John Buchan who generally regarded Muslims as a threat to European civilization. Lewis was more a Little Englander than an imperialist; I don't think Lewis ever cites Kipling approvingly. The modern literature Lewis read, instead, was replete with Islamic stereotypes. Even if he has the face of a Hindu deity, Lewis' "Tash the inexorable, the irresistible" owes a great deal to a conception of the Islamic God that he found elsewhere among his countrymen: in the face of this deity's will, human beings can do no other than bow and submit.

It is no good denying that Shasta's foster father Arsheesh and the Calormene Tarkaan who barters with him for his adopted son are anything other than Arabs out of nineteenth-century English fantasy. What they are doing, of course, is bartering for Shasta's soul, and selling or buying him into slavery. The Calormenes make their first onstage appearance in the Narnia series in *The Voyage of the "Dawn Treader,"* as merchants purchasing slaves from pirates; they have lost their money after the rough batch of Pevensies and talking mice were freed by Prince Caspian. "They wear flowing robes and orange-coloured turbans, and they are a wise, wealthy, courteous, cruel and ancient people."[17] They speak in long and polite proverbs, but these merchants coldly and persistently require their money back for the slaves freed from the auction block.

The Calormenes are not, in Lewis' imagination, simply a slaveholding people. Slavery is not a peculiar institution in Calormene society. All of them are slaves through and through, from the Grand Vizier down to the merest peasant who must jump out of the way of cutting whips as he navigates the Tashbaan traffic. After inadvertently eavesdropping on her betrothed's conversation, Aravis describes

---

[17] *The Voyage of the "Dawn Treader,"* 451–52, chap. 4.

the Grand Vizier as a "hideous groveling slave who flatters when he's kicked."[18] When Shasta likewise inadvertently spies out the Narnian plans to give Prince Rabadash the slip, he thinks, "I simply daren't tell them I'm not Prince Corin *now*.... I've heard all their plans. If they knew I wasn't one of themselves, they'd never let me out of this house alive. They'd be afraid I'd betray them to the Tisroc. They'd kill me. And if the real Corin turns up, it'll come out, and they *will*!" The narrator adds, "He had, you see, no idea how noble and free-born people behave."[19]

There are a few digs at Calormene voluntarist theology, but the point of the contrast of the Narnians and the Calormenes is sociological, anthropological, and moral; it is to contrast a free society with a society of slaves. Calormene society is one in which everyone values their own autonomy and seeks mainly to achieve power over others, and in which everyone, right up to the Tisroc, is a slave.

From Slavery to Freedom

We can often grasp the meaning of a book from the title. It doesn't always work when the book has been translated from the German. But more often than not, perhaps, the author distills his idea into five or six words at the front, and one can indeed judge a book by that part of its cover. The horse of *The Horse and His Boy* does not belong to Shasta and is not the "Boy's Horse," because he is a free Narnian horse; he does not exist for human use and exploitation. This idea makes complete, intuitive sense to a child. Narnia spells and symbolizes "freedom" because the talking animals are their own people, free persons. This is spelled out several times by the horses themselves.

[18] *The Horse and His Boy*, 257, chap. 8.
[19] Ibid., 239, chap. 5.

When Aravis asks Bree and Shasta why they keep talking to "her" horse instead of to her, even her gentle mare objects: " 'Excuse me, Tarkheena,' said Bree (with just the slightest backward tilt of his ears), 'but that's Calormene talk. We're free Narnians, Hwin and I, and I suppose, if you're running away to Narnia, you want to be free too. In that case Hwin isn't *your* horse any longer. One might just as well say you're *her* human.' "[20] The idea that, even in our world, the four-legged animals do not exist to be instrumentalized and exploited by human beings mattered a lot to C. S. Lewis. It is a significant point in the third volume of his adult Space Trilogy, *That Hideous Strength*, where evil scientists kidnap animals to experiment on them. In *The Horse and His Boy*, Lewis uses that same idea to represent the contrast of a society of free persons and a slave society. Bree is not going to pretend that the Tisroc could or should "live forever": " 'Why?' asked the Horse. 'I'm a free Narnian. And why should I talk slaves' and fools' talk? I don't want him to live forever, and I know that he's not going to live forever whether I want him to or not. And I can see you're from the free North too. No more of this Southern jargon between you and me.' "[21]

Above and beyond representing a slave society, Calormen represents *captivity*. In that sense, the point of it is not just moral but downright theological. Deciding that it is not really "stealing" to take money from the Tarkaan's saddlebag, Bree observes, "A free horse and a talking horse mustn't steal, of course. But I think it's all right. We're prisoners and captives in enemy country. That money is booty, spoil. Besides, how are we to get any food for you without it?"[22] Lewis wants to imply that all of us here on earth, outside of Christ, are prisoners and captive to the devil. Human nature, fallen from its original paradise, is in a condition of slavery and lives in an infernal region of captivity. The downfall of pride and the triumph of humility are not, in *The Horse and His Boy*, a simple moral fable; pride represents slavery to the demonic powers, and the humble soul is the soul freed and released from whining servitude.

The Longing for Return

The neo-Platonic theme of an ascending return to a forsaken paradise from which we once came is stamped in Lewis' imagination; this is a large part of what he means by its "baptism" (by George MacDonald). This is why he so disliked reductionist explanations of human desire, or what he called "Bulverism," named after the revelation that occurred to the fictional Ezekiel Bulver when he heard his mother tell his father that arithmetical formula are merely patriarchal constructions. Much of Lewis' early book, *The Pilgrim's Regress*, is heavy-handed mockery of reductionist explanations of desires, such as the then-fashionable bargain-basement Freudian interpretations of human behavior. Lewis thought reductionism was exactly the reverse of the truth; our ideas and desires are *more* than we can conceive, and not less.

Freud had coined the term "Oedipus complex," to explain human desires by reference to the dreadfully accurate prophecies about Sophocles' hero. I wonder if Shasta's origin story is a deliberate inversion of Oedipus'

[22] Ibid., 214, chap. 2.

story—about whom it is foretold, as a baby, that he will do evil, but whose parents' efforts to kill him are thwarted by a kindly servant and a shepherd. In the case of baby Cor, a centaur prophesies that he will save Archenland, so an evil lord kidnaps him and takes him away by sea to Calormen, dying himself on the way. We are more like Cor. The prophecy originally written on our hearts is to achieve greatness, not evil. Sophocles may have been speaking of the human condition as it is now, as what a Christian would call "fallen," rather than of man in his essence. But Lewis is not writing against Sophocles; he is writing against Freud as an all-consuming interpreter of human nature.

Returning to the Autobiographical Quality of *The Horse and His Boy*

None of the Pevensies, nor Jill, nor even Eustace Scrubb *is* C. S. Lewis in the way that Shasta is. The uneducated, unmannered boy from the fisherman's cottage who sulked in the face of Aravis's well-bred refinement is the adult Lewis who always felt a bumbler and an alien in this world. The journey from Calormen to Narnia is the spiritual journey that Lewis undertook from his prosaic childhood in Belfast to the "Joy" of Christianity. This analogue was present in Lewis' mind as he wrote the book. When Hwin meets the King of the Beasts in the hermit's garden in Archenland, Aslan says, "Dearest daughter,... I knew you would not be long in coming to me. Joy shall be yours."[23]

In *Surprised by Joy*, Lewis contrasts the prosaic character of his parents' literary tastes as compared to his own. Both his parents loved to read: his mother read solid,

[23] Ibid., 299, chap. 14.

down-to-earth Victorian novels; his father adored the political fiction of Trollope, rhetoric, affective poetry, and the English comedic tradition exemplified by Dickens. His father was, Lewis recalls,

> almost without rival, the best *raconteur* I have ever heard.... What neither he nor my mother had the least taste for was that kind of literature to which my allegiance was given the moment I could choose books for myself. Neither had ever listened for the horns of elfland. There was no copy either of Keats or Shelley in the house.... If I am a romantic my parents bear no responsibility for it.[24]

Lewis' parents gave him a great deal. He would have been a novelist like George MacDonald, who is seldom today read for pleasure, if he had not inherited his father's skills as a *raconteur* and thus the ability to "do" the characters and their voices. The great tradition of the English comic novel flows into and irrigates the Narnia books, raising them, in my view, even above Middle Earth. Nonetheless, just as Arsheesh's lack of interest in "the beyond" is contrasted with Shasta's dreams about what lies to the north, so Lewis' parents' enjoyment of this-worldly literature contrasts with his own.

One of the most famous passages in *Surprised by Joy* is the origin story of "Joy" itself, as Lewis understands it. Next to his working-class nurse, Lizzie, the other great blessing of Lewis' early life was, he says,

> my brother.... We were very different. Our earliest pictures ... reveal it. His were of ships and trains and battles; mine ... were of what we both called "dressed animals"— the anthropomorphized beasts of nursery literature. His

[24] *Surprised by Joy*, 10.

earliest story ... was called *The Young Rajah*. He had already made India "his country"; Animal-Land was mine.... But nowhere, either in my brother's work or my own, is there a single line drawn in obedience to an idea, however crude, of beauty.... This absence of beauty ... is characteristic of our childhood. No picture on the walls of our father's house ever attracted—and indeed none deserved—our attention. We never saw a beautiful building nor imagined that a building could be beautiful. My earliest aesthetic experiences ... were already incurably romantic. Once in those very early days my brother brought into the nursery the lid of a biscuit tin which he had covered with moss and garnished with twigs and flowers so as to make it a toy garden or a toy forest. This was the first beauty I ever knew.... I do not think the impression was very important at the moment, but it soon became important in memory. As long as I live my imagination of Paradise will retain something of my brother's toy garden. And every day there were what we called "the Green Hills" ... the low line of the Castlereagh Hills which we saw from the nursery windows. They were not very far off but they were, to children, quite unattainable. They taught me longing—*Sehnsucht*; made me for good or ill, and before I was six years old, a votary of the Blue Flower.[25]

When Lewis says he was a votary of the Blue Flower, that means that he longs for what seems unattainable; he was addicted to what he elsewhere calls "inconsolable longing."[26] Lewis was by his Ulster origins and lifelong Anglicanism preserved from the attentions of the Holy Office, but he is speaking of what the Jesuits of his own generation called "the natural desire for the supernatural vision."

[25] Ibid., 10–12.
[26] Ibid., 61–62.

Along with those luminaries, he realized from his own experience that the peoples of his time, who had lived through the Great War, would not return to the faith through moral exhortation, but only through rediscovering that their hearts are restless and joyless until they find enjoyment and rest in God.

Just like Shasta, Lewis can see the hills from the window of his house, and as with the fisherman's son, the sight of the hills taught him to long for and desire joy. His desire for joy is not expressed in his stories about "Animal Land," however. Lewis' Animal Land was not a childhood version of Narnia. It was, he says a bit further on in *Surprised by Joy*, utterly prosaic, and had nothing in common with Narnia except the anthropomorphic beasts. Animal Land excluded the least hint of wonder. Lewis' glimpses of joy taught him to fill Animal Land with wonder and mystery. They also taught him to plant Narnia in the North.

Narnia and the North: Joy

The persistent refrain of *The Horse and His Boy* is "Now for Narnia and the North!"[27] And the reason is autobiographical: Lewis came to associate joy with Northernness through his discovery, first, of Norse myth and then of Wagner. He says that Wagner would lead him to Northern mythology. Lewis comes to give Northernness a definite article: "*the* Northernness" is "essentially a desire and implied the absence of its object."[28] Whenever he mentions it, Lewis speaks of cold Northern skies:

[27] See *The Horse and His Boy*, 212, chap. 1.
[28] *Surprised by Joy*, 1985, 69.

I had become fond of Longfellow's *Saga of King Olaf*....
But ... there came a moment when I idly turned the pages
... and found the unrhymed translation of *Tegner's Drapa*
and read

> I had heard a voice that cried,
> Balder, the beautiful
> Is dead, is dead—.

I knew nothing about Balder; but instantly I was uplifted
into huge regions of northern sky, I desired with almost
sickening intensity something never to be described ...
and then ... found myself at the very same moment already
falling of that desire and wishing I were back in it.[29]

Lewis is about eight years old when he first discovers Balder. There are then five or more years of one-
dimensional boarding-school experience until

this long winter broke up in a single moment.... What I
had read was the words of *Siegfried and the Twilight of the
Gods*. What I had seen was one of Arthur Rackham's illustrations to that volume. I had never heard of Wagner, nor
of Siegfried. I thought the Twilight of the Gods was the
twilight in which the gods lived.... Pure "Northernness"
engulfed me: a vision of huge, clear spaces hanging over
the Atlantic in the endless twilight of Northern summer,
remoteness, severity ... and almost at the same moment
I knew that I had met this before, long, long ago ... in
Tegner's Drapa.... And with that plunge back into my
own past there arose at once, almost like heartbreak, the
memory of Joy itself, the knowledge that I had once had
what I had now lacked for years, *that I was returning at last
from exile and desert lands to my own country*; and the distance
of the Twilight of the Gods and the distance of my own
past Joy, both unattainable, flowed together into a single,
unendurable sense of desire and loss.[30]

[29] Ibid., 19–20.
[30] Ibid., 62 (italics added).

These lines seem to contain the key not only to *The Horse and His Boy* but to Lewis' apologetics. "I was returning at last from exile and desert lands to my own country." This is of course the heart of the novel, and the heart of Lewis' conception of Christianity.

He had as yet to hear a single note of Wagner: "Next holidays, in the dark crowded shop of T. Edens Osborne ... I first heard a record of the *Ride of the Valkyries....* To a boy already crazed with 'the Northernness,' whose highest musical experience had been Sullivan, the *Ride* came like a thunderbolt."

We must be clear that for Lewis the imaginative and literary "Joy" which is induced by aesthetic experiences is not one and the same thing as the beatific vision. It is not even precisely a foretaste of it. It is God's tackle and lure, God's unsubtle "clickbait"; the pursuit of joy is what leads Lewis, unknowingly, toward heaven and true freedom. Lewis writes, "On my cousin's dressing table I found the very book which had started the whole affair.... *Siegfried and the Twilight of the Gods* illustrated by Arthur Rackham. His pictures, which seemed to me then to be the very music made visible, plunged me a few fathoms deeper into my delight.... I [was] enslaved by Northernness."[31] You can still be a slave to joy, and the pursuit of joy can become idolatrous, because the joyous vision of Arthur Rackham's illustrations is only an image of the vision of God. But Lewis continues:

> At the time, Asgard and the Valkyries seemed to me ... more important than anything else.... They seemed much more important than my growing doubts about Christianity.... If the Northernness seemed then a bigger thing than my religion, that may ... have been because my attitude towards it contained elements which my religion ought to

[31] Ibid., 64.

have contained and did not.... There was in it something very like adoration, some kind of quite disinterested self-abandonment to an object which securely claimed this by simply being the object it was.... Sometimes I can almost think that I was sent back to the false gods there to acquire some capacity for worship against the day when the true God should recall me to Himself.[32]

The Movement of Divine Providence Runs North

So *The Horse and His Boy* is not about a boy who is simply lured by the longing for liberty and romance to the free and romantic North. Like supernatural desire, the North-ernness is a *calling* and a vocation. Shasta does not jump for the North, when he runs away with Bree; he is drawn. All through the story, we learn, he has been pushed and pro-pelled northward by Aslan himself. When Shasta encoun-ters a shadowy but massive presence in the dark forest, and tells that strange presence his sob story, he is not met with immediate sympathy:

> "Don't you think it was bad luck to meet so many lions?" asked Shasta....
> "There was only one: but he was swift of foot.... I was the lion who forced you to join with Aravis. And I was the cat who comforted you among the houses of the dead. I was the lion who drove the jackals from you while you slept. I was the lion who gave the Horses the new strength of fear for the last mile so that you should reach King Lune in time. And I was the lion who pushed the boat in which you lay, a child near death, so that it came to shore where a man sat, wakeful at midnight, to receive you." ...

[32] Ibid., 65.

"Who *are you*?" asked Shasta.

"Myself," said the Voice, very deep and low so that the earth shook: and again, "Myself" loud and clear and gay: and then the third time "Myself" whispered so softly you could hardly hear it, and yet it seemed to come from all round you.[33]

Aslan could equally say, "I was the inconsolable longing; I was your desire to escape; I am the North."

[33] *The Horse and His Boy*, 281, chap. 11.

VI

THE MAGICIAN'S NEPHEW

On Knowing Him Here for a Little

Part VI

Madeline Infantine

To know him is to know the song begins:
the blackness overhead ablaze with stars,
the one who cuts through dark where none has
    been.

New stars with new voices belt harmonies shared,
constellations and planets sing praises and prayers.

Here is the first stir of fresh wind,
the steady slow sky, the green-gilded hills,
and pink and gold sunlight.

Currant comes flowering, finding the earth soft,
beeches murmur to us: listen, watch.

Bless the bristle grass,
the dark heather growth,
the wild roses and the rhododendron.

Where once was only silence, kindly song:
braying mare, yelping mouse,
barking hound, thumping beaver.

His, the gift of woods and rivers,
yours, the watching,
yours, the listening.

Come, with your mouth open, your eyes shining.
Come, singing hymns of praise
to him, giver of stars and self.

His is the song that sings all into being,
the call that rings in all our singing.

The Magician's Nephew:
A Mystagogical Story of Creation

Catherine Rose Cavadini

In the beginning, when God created the heavens and the
   earth,
the earth was a formless wasteland, and darkness covered
   the abyss, while a mighty wind swept over the waters.
Then God said,
"Let there be light," and there was light.
                                God saw how good the light was.

                                            —Genesis 1:1–4[1]

The eastern sky changed from white to pink and from
pink to gold. The Voice rose and rose, till all the air was
shaking with it. And just as it swelled to the mightiest and
most glorious sound it had yet produced, the sun arose.

                                — *The Magician's Nephew*, chap. 8

C. S. Lewis' beautiful description of Aslan singing Narnia into creation reflects the biblical account of creation
in Genesis 1. Lewis' story and Genesis 1 both declare the

---

[1] New American Bible, © 2002 Confraternity of Christian Doctrine. I cite
this translation throughout the chapter due to its use in the Catholic Mass in
the United States.

love that brought about the creation of the world. I aim to compare and harmonize these two accounts of creation, while also examining some particular responses to creation, described by the characters in Lewis' story and encouraged by the Catholic liturgical and contemplative life. Finally, I will ask how these accounts of creative love can elucidate the responses of gratitude and self-sacrifice that are appropriate to such love. Put most simply, I suggest reading *The Magician's Nephew* as a mystagogical story of sainthood—a story about learning to live in the mystery of God's creative love.

Narnia's Genesis

As with the accounts in Genesis, Lewis' reader is invited in *The Magician's Nephew* to envision the act of creation. Here, though, we are helped with this vision more than in Genesis because we have the reactions of those truly observing Aslan's creative work to assist our imagination. (And some editions also have illustrations!) This does not mean that creation, for Lewis, is any less of a mystery, just that he invites our imaginations to explore it more deeply.

As we already noted, Aslan "sings" Narnia into existence. The sons and daughters of Adam, who have coincidentally arrived in Narnia at just this moment, watch and listen. In the darkness (or "nothing") before Narnia's beginning, Uncle Andrew, the Cabby, Polly, and Digory all hear Aslan singing, aware of the song before encountering the singer or witnessing the song's effects:

> A voice had begun to sing. It was very far away and Digory found it hard to decide from what direction it was coming.... It was, beyond comparison, the most beautiful noise

he had ever heard. It was so beautiful he could hardly bear
it.... Then two wonders happened at the same moment.
One was that the voice was suddenly joined by other voices;
more voices than you could possibly count. They were in
harmony with it, but far higher up the scale: cold, tingling,
silvery voices. The second was that the blackness overhead,
all at once, was blazing with stars.... It was the stars themselves that were singing, and ... it was the First Voice ...
which had made them appear and made them sing.[2]

Polly's observations are helpful in drawing out the connection between this song and the creative activity witnessed as the skies and earth erupted with light and life:
"When [the Lion] burst into a rapid series of lighter notes
[Polly] was not surprised to see primroses suddenly appearing in every direction. Thus, with an unspeakable thrill,
she felt quite certain that all the things were coming (as
she said) 'out of the Lion's head.' When you listened to the
Lion's song, you heard the things he was making up: when
you looked round you, you saw them."[3] Aslan truly thinks
and sings Narnia into existence, beautiful and luminous
through his song!

This account of Narnian creation gives readers a fresh
take on God separating the light from the darkness in
Scripture's first Creation account. In Genesis 1, God simply says, "Let there be light" and then "there was light"
(Gen 1:3). There is no rosy, luminous sunrise in Genesis. But the message of both is the same: the goodness of
creation revealing the goodness of the Creator. With his
literary efforts, Lewis reminds readers that Scripture's cos-
mology directs us toward God. Leon Kass' commentary
on Genesis is instructive in this regard: "Heaven and its

---

[2] *The Magician's Nephew*, 61, chap. 8.
[3] Ibid., 65, chap. 9.

occupants are not eternal, they come into being; there is something temporally before, causally behind, and ontologically above the cosmos.... Heaven, the enduring vault of the cosmos, the stunning star-studded sphere that ceaselessly circles above and to which ancient people looked with awe and fear, wonder and admiration, is, according to the Bible, not deserving of such respect."[4] But God is.

The creature is meant to be in awe of God, and to praise Him. Indeed, the creation is a "space," as Pope Benedict XVI puts it, that God made such that "he might communicate his love, and from which the response of love might come back to him."[5] Following Scripture, Lewis invites readers to think along the contours of God's creative thought, and to sing, as it were, the song of love that conforms us to love's creative reality—to what Genesis might call God's *dominion of love*. This dominion is extended to us at our creation in Genesis: "Then God said: 'Let us make man in our image, after our likeness. Let them have dominion ...'" (Gen 1:26). We participate properly in God's dominion by listening and responding to God's creative call: Let them have dominion *in our image*!

In *The Magician's Nephew*, the characters who watch and respond to Aslan's song image various responses to God: one good, one evil, and one in need of transformation. A close look at all three will set in view, under Aslan's sun, the path to sainthood, the mystagogical journey. Let us look now at the responses given by the Cabby, Uncle Andrew, and Digory.

[4] Leon R. Kass, *The Beginning of Wisdom: Reading Genesis* (Chicago: University of Chicago Press, 2006), 40.

[5] Benedict XVI, Homily for the Easter Vigil (April 23, 2011), https://www.vatican.va/content/benedict-xvi/en/homilies/2011/documents/hf_ben-xvi_hom_20110423_veglia-pasquale.html.

Watching and Listening, Take One: The Cabby

The Cabby's response to Aslan's song is pure doxology—
pure praise—and he images what the right response to
God makes of a person: a saint according to God's dominion of love.

The Cabby watches Aslan and listens to his song with
"shining eyes" and "open mouth," "drinking in the
sound."[6] He watches and listens, fully engrossed by the
love that is singing such beauty into existence right before
his eyes. His whole response is captured in his first words
as he sees the blackness of the not-sky become the blazing
realm of singing stars: "Glory be!"[7] The response of the
Cabby is one of awe and gratitude, of praise and thanksgiving. The Cabby is simply and purely doxological.

Gratitude is the one response that allows our dominion
to be exercised—dominion that has first and foremost to
do with our own creation and conversion. We see this
connection between gratitude and dominion in the transformation that comes over the Cabby. In this utterance of
a "Glory be!" the Cabby becomes Frank, the first king of
Narnia: "All the sharpness and cunning and quarrelsome-
ness which he had picked up as a London cabby seemed
to have been washed away, and the courage and kindness
which he had always had were easier to see. Perhaps it
was the air of the young world that had done it, or talking
with Aslan, or both."[8] Even the Cabby's horse, now transformed into the talking and flying Fledge, recognized the
noble change in his master: "My old master's been changed
nearly as much as I have! Why, he's a real master now."[9]

[6] *The Magician's Nephew*, 62, chap. 8.
[7] Ibid.
[8] Ibid., 96, chap. 14.
[9] Ibid., 97, chap. 14.

We might draw on the Book of Revelation to add to Fledge's description. Frank is washed, robed, and crowned, a truly "living creature," giving "glory and honor and thanks" (Rev 4:9). Frank has been given the gift of dominion. And how did all of this come about? As Lewis shows, simply by "talking with Aslan"—that is, by entering into the dialogue of creation. The call and response of Creator and creation invites conversion and mastery over our own selves. Together, dominion is exercised over our transformation into saints.

This simple and shining example of doxological response and dominion provides us perspective for looking at the divergent response of Uncle Andrew, and then the response of Digory as he struggles toward transformation.

Watching and Listening, Take Two: Uncle Andrew

Uncle Andrew offers quite a contrast to the Cabby-turned-King. Throughout the creation of Narnia, Uncle Andrew is told again and again by the Cabby to "stow it" because "watchin' and listenin's the thing now!"[10] In this way, the Cabby voices the words of the prophet Isaiah: "Come to me heedfully, listen" (Is 55:3). But Uncle Andrew is unwilling to be quiet, watch, and listen. We learn right away that Uncle Andrew does not exercise dominion over himself. As a result, he cannot see Aslan's creative activity for what it is: an expression of love. Uncle Andrew isn't interested in the "magic" of loving. He is only interested in being a "magician" himself, of exercising some other self-loving power.

[10] Ibid., 65, chap. 9.

We can see this response in Uncle Andrew's posture toward Aslan's creative song. As Uncle Andrew watched Aslan sing, his "mouth was open" like the Cabby's, "but not open with joy," not to drink in the almost unbearable beauty appearing and sounding around him. Rather, Uncle Andrew "looked more as if his chin had simply dropped away from the rest of his face. His shoulders were stooped and his knees shook. He was not liking the Voice. If he could have got away from it by creeping into a rat's hole, he would have done so."[11]

Lewis' description of Uncle Andrew is quite comical. How ridiculous Uncle Andrew seems as the reader moves along, especially in contrast to King Frank. But perhaps this comic relief gives greater agency to Lewis' example of Uncle Andrew, for we are all like Uncle Andrew sometimes, and Lewis makes it easier to hear this with some levity and laughter. *We* need to be shown how the dominion of love allows for the reality of sin—for our not wanting very much to hear "the Voice" speaking to us, for our reluctance and dejectedness. And sometimes we only become willing to "watch and listen" from a "rat's hole."

There are two further comic ways in which the story of Uncle Andrew and his dominion of self-love unfolds. First, readers watch as he wishes to exercise dominion over Narnia, but for his own personal gain, as if the whole new world had just been created for his own use. Uncle Andrew would like to commercialize Narnia's creative powers and become a millionaire. Only one thing stands in his way: "that brute," the singing Lion.[12]

In short, Uncle Andrew would like to kill Aslan—"that brute"—and thereby replace God with himself. And it

[11] Ibid., 62, chap. 8.
[12] See ibid., 67–68, chap. 9.

will seemingly "cost" Andrew "nothing." This is the classic definition of sin, from its very origin, and as described in Genesis 3. "You will be like gods," promises the serpent. Sin is the opposite of gratitude. It is to see the world through wholly me-colored glasses. "Glory be ... to *me!*" Andrew exercises no Aslan-like dominion over himself. He is unwilling even to pay the price of *seeing* anything worthy of love and attention beyond himself—neither, we are told, his sad nephew Digory, nor Digory's dying mother who is his own sister. In all of this, Andrew only participates in becoming less himself, ceding the dominion of love to selfish pride.

This brings us to Lewis' second comical picture of Uncle Andrew. The talking animals of the new Narnia make Uncle Andrew their pet. This great magician, capable, so he thinks, of becoming a godlike, magical, and ingenious millionaire, has been reduced to an incomprehensible beast. This is illustrated in the way the talking animals cannot understand Uncle Andrew's speech and adopt him. The Narnian animals, writes Lewis, "were really getting quite fond of their strange pet and hoped that Aslan would allow them to keep it. The cleverer ones were quite sure by now that at least some of the noises which came out of its mouth had a meaning. They christened him Brandy because he made that noise so often."[13]

Perhaps the only element more ridiculous in Lewis' depiction of Uncle Andrew is how Andrew himself perceives the creative activity happening around him. His thoughts are now in stark contrast to Aslan's thoughts. Uncle Andrew is centered on Andrew rather than the Creator. Andrew is not being transformed into a saint,

[13] Ibid., 98, chap. 14.

but into a dumb beast. He refuses the dominion of love. Lewis hereby opens a window onto another unobservable phenomenon: the *un*creation of Andrew as he refuses to respond to Aslan, or even to hear Aslan's song:

> "Of course it can't really have been singing," [Uncle Andrew] thought, "I must have imagined it. I've been letting my nerves get out of order. Who ever heard of a lion singing?" And the longer and more beautiful the Lion sang, the harder Uncle Andrew tried to make himself believe that he could hear nothing but roaring. Now the trouble about trying to make yourself stupider than you really are is that you very often succeed. Uncle Andrew did. He soon did hear nothing but roaring in Aslan's song. Soon he couldn't have heard anything else even if he had wanted to. And when at last the Lion spoke and said, "Narnia awake," he didn't hear any words: he heard only a snarl. And when the Beasts spoke in answer, he heard only barkings, growlings, bayings, and howlings. And when they laughed—well, you can imagine. That was worse for Uncle Andrew than anything that had happened yet. Such a horrid, bloodthirsty din of hungry and angry brutes he had never heard in his life.[14]

Reluctant to see reality for what it is, Uncle Andrew is unable to imagine the real dominion of love or to aspire to sainthood. Aslan himself pronounces the tragedy and ludicrousness of Andrew's downfall: "He has made himself unable to hear my voice. If I spoke to him, he would hear only growlings and roarings. Oh Adam's sons, how *cleverly* you defend yourselves against all that might do you *good*!"[15]

[14] Ibid., 75–76, chap. 10.
[15] Ibid., 98, chap. 14 (italics added).

Watching and Listening, Take Three: Digory

Finally, we arrive at the response of Digory, which reveals the transformative—or mystagogical—journey toward sainthood. His response encompasses his decision to speak to Aslan; his journey to retrieve the apple; and his struggle to withstand the temptation to take this apple home for his dying mother, remember Aslan's love, and bring the apple in sacrifice and thanksgiving to Aslan. By composing this narrative of Digory's strenuous transformation, Lewis provides his readers with the images and the courage to imagine that becoming a saint is a very real possibility for everyone.

When his creative song falls silent, Aslan stops to gaze upon the beasts, breathe a long warm breath upon them, and make them Talking Beasts: "Narnia, Narnia, Narnia, awake. Love. Think. Speak."[16] Love is the framework for thinking and speaking (or acting). Narnia is instructed to awaken to love and to see all things through love.

Digory himself also awakens in this moment to love, heeding love's logic, and the dialogue of love opens. He awakens to the love that he has just witnessed constituting everything around him. Digory is in awe, and in his awe he follows Aslan, unable to take his eyes off the ever more golden Lion.

Digory's encounter with Aslan will make him ready to "love, think, and speak." This transformation begins when Digory first talks with Aslan, pleading for help on behalf of his dying mother. What the desperate and despairing Digory encounters in the Lion startles him: "For the tawny face was bent down near his own and (wonder of wonders) great shining tears stood in the Lion's eyes. They were such big, bright tears compared with Digory's own

---

[16] Ibid., 70, chap. 9.

that for a moment he felt as if the Lion must really be sor-
rier about his Mother than he was himself." Aslan, with
a pure grief, uncolored by anything selfish, entered into
Digory's despair. Digory is surprised by this great love—it
is "a wonder of wonders."

The dialogue continues with Aslan calling Digory to his
mission on behalf of Narnia:

> "My son, my son," said Aslan, "I know. Grief is great.
> Only you and I in this land know that yet. Let us be good
> to one another. But I have to think of hundreds of years
> in the life of Narnia. The Witch whom you have brought
> into this world will come back to Narnia again. But it
> need not be yet. It is my wish to plant in Narnia a tree that
> she will not dare to approach, and that tree will protect
> Narnia from her for many years.... You must get me the
> seed from which that tree is to grow."
>
> "Yes, sir," said Digory.

And Lewis adds that Digory "didn't quite know how it
was to be done but he felt quite sure now that he would be
able to do it. The Lion drew a deep breath, stooped its head
even lower and gave him a Lion's kiss. And at once Digory
felt that new strength and courage had gone into him."[17]

With Aslan's tears and a kiss, Digory's mystagogical
journey begins. On this journey, Digory will learn to
love as Aslan loves, eventually making his own sacrifice of
thanksgiving. Thus encouraged and sustained, Digory sets
out across Narnia to retrieve the silver apple that will protect Narnia from the witch Jadis. Along the way, Digory is
further strengthened by the beauty and goodness of Narnia, all of which arose from the Lion's song, and continue
to reveal Aslan's dominion of love to Digory.

[17] Ibid., 83–84, chap. 12.

However, in the Eden-like garden of the silver apples, Digory also finds Jadis. Snakelike, Jadis tempts Digory with the silver apple of life, testing his love for Aslan and inviting him to revise his response to the Lion:

> "But what about this Mother of yours whom you *pretend* to love so?... Do you not see, Fool, that one bite of that apple would heal her? You have it in your pocket. We are here by ourselves and the Lion is far away. Use your Magic and go back to your own world. A minute later you can be at your Mother's bedside, give her the fruit. Five minutes later you will see the color coming back to her face. She will tell you the pain is gone. Soon she will tell you she feels stronger. Then she will fall asleep—think of that; hours of sweet natural sleep, without pain, without drugs. Next day everyone will be saying how wonderfully she has recovered. Soon she will be quite well again. All will be well again. Your home will be happy again. You will be like other boys."
>
> "Oh!" gasped Digory as if he had been hurt, and put his hand to his head. For he now knew that the most terrible choice lay before him.[18]

The terrible choice before Digory was whether to think, act, and love according to Aslan's tears or, instead, according to his own. Digory must discern between love and pretending to love. He must come to understand the tears of Aslan better and better—mystagogically.

As the dialogue continues, the Witch presents Aslan as a pitiless master who seeks to make Digory his slave. She tells of a Lion who does not care about Digory's grief, who is leading the boy to turn away from his mother's pain and is making *him* heartless in the process. Even in the fog of her accusations, Digory knows this tale to be untrue. He

[18] Ibid., 93–94, chap. 13.

remembers the Lion's tears and he feels how his conversation with Aslan made him *courageous* rather than heartless. His heart has grown, not shrunk. His heart has been stretching toward the size of the Lion's heart—the Lion who showed so much sorrow for Digory's mother that Digory's own sorrow seemed small by comparison. He discerns that it is the Witch who is cruel and pitiless. She tempts Digory with his concern for his mother and with his own despair.

Coming into dominion over himself in this moment means resisting the Witch's temptation to doubt Aslan and to forget the love expressed in his big, bright tears and his songs of joy. As he journeys more deeply into Aslan's love, into Aslan's dominion, Digory learns that his love for his mother is truly but a sign and reference point for divine love. Indeed, a mother's love can teach us about God's love for us; Scripture uses motherhood as an analogical sign (cf. Is 49:15). A mother's love points us beyond itself, to the truest, freest love of all: God's love. God's love truly "mothers" us; God creates us, frees us, and redeems us in love.

Jadis' logic runs contrary to such creative and redemptive love. Her logic even suggests Digory is not free: He should not bring the apple to Aslan, for this would not be an act of love. It might even condemn his mother to her death. What *would* his mother think, after all? Yet Digory, in beholding this difficult choice, realizes that he *is* free—he has the dominion—to think and speak and love according to a larger, truer love.[19] Aslan's love has mothered him and

---

[19] Two quotes from Lewis' *The Four Loves* make the point: "We may give our human loves the unconditional allegiance which we owe only to God. Then they become gods: then they become demons [or witches]. Then they will destroy [or uncreate] us." Further, Lewis adds, "All human beings pass away. Do not let your happiness depend on something you may lose. If love is to be a blessing, not a misery, it must be for the only Beloved who will never pass away." C. S. Lewis, *The Four Loves* (San Francisco: HarperOne, 2017), 152–54.

given him the capacity to choose how he himself will love: according to true love, to divine love.

We can see now that turning to listen and respond to the Witch would bring Digory into her dominion. But this would only bring greater misery and despair, for her dominion is a heartless dominion. It would bring destruction to Digory and to Narnia, as it did to Charn (the "dying" world where we first meet Jadis as Queen). She cannot bring an Easter morning into the heart.

Thus confronted by Jadis while holding to the memory of Aslan's tears, Digory enters the dominion of love. He chooses the mystagogical path that leads to sanctity: "Digory never spoke on the way back [to Aslan], and the others were shy of speaking to him. He was very sad and he wasn't even sure all the time that he had done the right thing; but whenever he remembered the shining tears in Aslan's eyes he became sure."[20] Because Aslan's tears express compassionate sorrow, they also express love and the possibility of joy. They express the fullness of the Creator's love for creation.

It is important that it is a memory of Aslan's tears that sustains Digory, strengthening him on his journey. Digory returns to his encounter with Aslan again and again, mystagogically plunging ever deeper into the reality of sacrificial love, receiving it again and again in his remembrance of those tears. Even once Aslan has Digory sent home with a silver apple in hand, and after his mother has eaten the apple and slept peacefully and awoken strengthened, Digory continues to remember his encounter with Aslan: "For the rest of that day, whenever he looked at the things about him, and saw how ordinary and unmagical they were, he hardly dared to hope, but when he remembered the face

[20] *The Magician's Nephew*, 95, chap. 13.

of Aslan he did hope."[21] Recalling thus the mysteries of
his own encounter with Aslan, and so the mysteries of his
creation and conversion, Digory is "awake" to the "other
kingdom" and conformed, day by day, memory by memory, to its dominion of love.

An Autobiographical Excursus

Digory's story is autobiographical, a vehicle for Lewis'
own experience of conversion, which unfolded between
the sorrow over his own mother's death as a young boy
and the "surprise," as Lewis called it, of real joy when God
descended into his heart many years later. Digory, as we
know, is focused on his mother's illness for much of *The
Magician's Nephew* and afraid of her death. He is crying as
the story begins, grubby and tearful. It is only when he
hears Aslan creating Narnia that the sad Digory is introduced to joy. As he watches the first sunrise, he hears the
sun "laugh for joy as it came up."[22] With our Lewis-like
Digory, then, we enter into the heart of the text's mystagogical journey because we enter into the unobservable
moment of Lewis' own creation and conversion.

Readers will notice, then, not only autobiographical,
but particularly mystagogical elements from Lewis' life
in Digory's story. In his autobiography, *Surprised by Joy*,
Lewis writes:

> You must picture me alone in that room in Magda-
> len, night after night, feeling, whenever my mind lifted
> even for a second from my work, the steady, unrelent-
> ing approach of Him whom I so earnestly desired not to

[21] Ibid., 104, chap. 15.
[22] Ibid., 62, chap. 8.

meet. That which I greatly feared had at last come upon
me. In the Trinity Term of 1929 I gave in, and admit-
ted that God was God, and knelt and prayed: perhaps,
that night, the most dejected and reluctant convert in all
England. I did not then see what is now the most shining
and obvious thing; the Divine humility which will accept
a convert even on such terms. The Prodigal Son at least
walked home on his own feet. But who can duly adore
that Love which will open the high gates to a prodigal
who is brought in kicking, struggling, resentful, and dart-
ing his eyes in every direction for a chance of escape?[23]

Though bereft of a single alleluia, this *is* a paschal
moment, a moment of "genesis." God approached Lewis
and descended into his struggle, into his resentment and his
reluctance. Elsewhere, though bereft of pinks and golds,
he describes this moment as a morning, much like that
first morning on which Aslan commanded Narnia, "Love.
Think. Speak." Lewis writes, "It was … like when a man,
after a long sleep, still lying motionless in bed, becomes
aware that he is now *awake*." Awake, Lewis looked and
saw "Christ and the other world of God's kingdom." He
looked back through his own history, through his memory, and discerned God's "unrelenting approach."[24]

This small window into Lewis' own journey reawakens
us to Digory in two new ways. First, it gives us an image
of Lewis' loving, thinking, and speaking. Second, it opens
the world of Narnia unto *our* liturgical and mystagogical
world. Lewis is remembering God's approach and, *in such
remembering*, wondering who can properly praise such a
love—who can so "duly adore" it? I will attempt a fuller
answer to Lewis' own question by linking *The Magician's
Nephew* to the Catholic liturgical and mystagogical life.

[23] *Surprised by Joy* (San Francisco: HarperCollins, 2017), 279.
[24] Ibid., 290. This is an Augustinian approach, as demonstrated throughout
his *Confessions*.

Liturgical Time, Mystagogy, and Sanctity

"In Christianity," as Pope John Paul II once wrote, "time has a fundamental importance. Within the dimension of time the world was created; within it the history of salvation unfolds, finding its culmination in the 'fullness of time' of the Incarnation."[25] Here we are particularly interested in the Christian belief that God works within time—within human history—to reveal himself to us, to give himself to us, and to invite us into his friendship.[26] The liturgical year, whose seasons commemorate the events of salvation history, celebrates this friendship with God while making our own history salvific. In the liturgy, each and every day, God continues to reveal himself and give himself to us in friendship.

The liturgy transcends the bounds of time, reaching both back into the moment of Christ's total gift, given once and for all, and into "the fullness of time." In the liturgy "Christ's today" intersects with the past, the present, and the future.[27] Liturgical time, therefore, transcends historical time and ceases to behave as one expects it to behave from a historical vantage point. Time behaves especially unexpectedly as Lewis' characters move between "our world" and the world of Narnia.

Contemplating the Easter celebration is helpful here. During the Easter Triduum (from the evening of Holy Thursday through the evening of Easter Sunday), we walk

---

[25] John Paul II, apostolic letter *Tertio millennio adveniente* (November 10, 1994), https://www.vatican.va/content/john-paul-ii/en/apost_letters/1994/documents/hf_jp-ii_apl_19941110_tertio-millennio-adveniente.html.

[26] See Vatican Council II, Dogmatic Constitution on Divine Revelation *Dei verbum* (November 18, 1965), no. 2, https://www.vatican.va/archive/hist_councils/ii_vatican_council/documents/vat-ii_const_19651118_dei-verbum_en.html.

[27] See Joseph Ratzinger, *The Spirit of the Liturgy*, Commemorative Edition (San Francisco: Ignatius Press, 2018), 67–75.

slowly with Christ through the historical moments of his Passion, Death, and Resurrection, so as to experience God's love in our own hearts. We are liturgically wed to this history and receive its transcendent and salvific effects. We find ourselves invited into God's friendship, we are offered God's divine Blood, and we are moved to respond. This is the first response in a lifelong process of gratitude.

The process of being conformed to God's love has a particular name and a particular liturgical season within Catholicism: mystagogy. Most properly, mystagogy is the fifty-day catechetical season for the newly baptized. During this season of mystagogical catechesis, the baptized seek to more deeply understand God's "will of love" as expressed and experienced in the liturgy and the sacraments. The mystagogue enters into the Church's remembrance and re-presentation of Christ's sacrifice of love.

And yet mystagogy is not simply a fifty-day task. It is truly the lifelong, ever deepening liturgical participation in the mystery of Christ. Mystagogy, then, is the lifelong conversion to holiness. Pope Benedict XVI put it beautifully: "What happens in baptism is the beginning of a process that embraces the whole of our life—it makes us fit for eternity, in such a way that, robed in the garment of light of Jesus Christ, we can appear before the face of God and live with him forever."[28]

The Easter Vigil and *The Magician's Nephew*

With the guiding light of the Easter Vigil, we can return to *The Magician's Nephew* to draw out the final harmonies

[28] Benedict XVI, Homily for the Easter Vigil (April 3, 2010), http://www.vatican.va/content/benedict-xvi/en/homilies/2010/documents/hf_ben-xvi_hom_20100403_veglia-pasquale.html.

between Genesis and the creation of Narnia in a mystagogical key.

The first reading for the Catholic Easter Vigil Mass
comes from the first creation account in Genesis 1, which
opens with these words: "In the beginning, when God
created the heavens and the earth ..." This opening
announces what the first creation account teaches above
all: that the proper approach to creation is to approach it
as a mystery. As we listen, the narrative is presented from
the perspective of someone watching and listening as God
creates. Yet it was not until the sixth day of creation that
anyone was created who could have watched or listened
or, therefore, narrated and written this account. In other
words, creation, in its "beginning," went unobserved and
was, in fact, unobservable. This, then, points to the mystery of Creation as an activity and a reality that arose from
the very heart of the Creator.[29]

That creation is a mystery is corroborated by other readings from the Easter Vigil, most notably that from Baruch
3 and Isaiah 55. Baruch, as heard at Mass, reads, "He who
dismisses the light, and it departs, calls it, and it obeys him
trembling; before whom the stars at their posts shine and
rejoice; he calls them, they answer, 'Here we are!' shining with joy for their Maker" (Bar 3:33–34). And Isaiah
55:10–11 tells us about God's creative word:

> For just as from the heavens
> the rain and snow come down
> and do not return there
> till they have watered the earth,
> making it fertile and fruitful,
> giving seed to the one who sows

---

[29] See John C. Cavadini, "Why Study God?," *Commonweal*, September 30,
2013, https://www.commonwealmagazine.org/why-study-god.

and bread to the one who eats,
so shall my word be
that goes forth from my mouth;
my word shall not return to me void,
but shall do my will,
achieving the end for which I sent it.

Thus Baruch and Isaiah both proclaim again that God created by speaking, developing a dialogue of call and response. "In the beginning" God *spoke* all things into existence, calling them with his eternal Word: "Let there be ..." And, because the Word is eternal, God is still calling us to become who we are; he calls us to "dominion."[30] And so the mystery of creation is not simply an unobservable event from the beginning of time, but the ongoing conversion of creation to the love that first moved God to "speak."

In the passage from Baruch, we also hear the stars respond to God, so glad in their new existence. This same idea of creation responding to the Creator's Word can be found in the original Hebrew of Genesis. When God calls to the earth to produce vegetation, he commands the grass "to grass."[31] Like the stars and the grass of Genesis, we are meant to respond to God who calls us to life. But we are the only creatures in Genesis who are "like God," made in God's image and given dominion over the rest of creation. Lewis' use of Genesis 1 in *The Magician's Nephew* shows us what it could look like to listen to God and to respond with dominion: conversion to the love that God "speaks" in his Word.

[30] For more on this understanding of God speaking us into existence, see Augustine, "The Literal Meaning of Genesis," in *The Works of Saint Augustine*, vol. 13, *On Genesis*, ed. John Rotelle, trans. Edmund Hill (Hyde Park, NY: New City Press, 2013), I.1–22.

[31] Kass, *The Beginning of Wisdom*, 49.

Our response to God is meant to image *God's* good dominion. Such a response is not easy. It is not like the grass grassing or the stars shining. As we see with Digory, responding to God is the process of "becoming" like God by loving more and more as God loves. It requires conversion. This can truly only happen if we listen and respond to God's call. "Come to me heedfully," says God in Isaiah 55:2–3, "listen, that you may have life."

As we already know, God has spoken to creation throughout history. Saint Augustine would add to this: God "spoke" most persuasively upon the Cross with his blood.[32] His blood testifies to the love of the Creator, "spoken" anew in the sacrificial *act* of his death. "No one has greater love than this, to lay down one's life for one's friends."[33] Thus, Genesis 1 finds its place in the Easter Liturgy, pointing us not only back to the beginning, but to the beginning that *today* can be, as we listen to our Creator and his Blood, speaking to us of love.

Aslan's blood "spoke" to us directly in *The Lion, the Witch and the Wardrobe* when Aslan gave his life in place of Edmund. We thus hear prophetic and sacrificial tones in the creation account of *The Magician's Nephew*. In one brief sentence in chapter 10, Aslan tells all the newly created talking creatures of Narnia, "I give you yourselves ... and I give you myself."[34] These are some of Aslan's first words to the Narnians, and they summarize salvation history, even though it is yet to unfold in Narnia, from the beginning to Easter Sunday and to every individual moment of "becoming" and conversion in the mystagogical journey of each creature. Aslan's gifts of "self" in creation—both

---

[32] See Augustine, *On Christian Teaching*, trans. D. W. Robertson, Jr. (Upper Saddle River, NJ: Prentice Hall, 1958), xli.

[33] Ibid.

[34] *The Magician's Nephew*, 71, chap. 10.

the gift of ourselves to us and of himself to us—help us understand the gift of dominion in Genesis. Self-gift is a way of entering more deeply into the mystery of Creation as explained by God's Death and Resurrection. Again, we hear Aslan in this way because our first experience was to come to Narnia through the wardrobe, long after Narnia's beginning. We are moving mystagogically!

A Conclusion: The Dominion of Love

Through *The Magician's Nephew*, Lewis draws his readers to the mystagogical path. Lewis' literary efforts inspire readers toward sainthood by imaging God's dominion of love. In contrast to Uncle Andrew's failed response to Aslan's call, the responses of Digory and King Frank help readers envision a good and grateful answer to God's "Let there be ..." The reader is likewise inspired to make God's love known in this world, and to make their history a liturgy.

As *The Magician's Nephew* suggests, mystagogical conversion leads to the dominion of love and thereby to sanctity precisely by remembering—every day and every week and every year—the love of God and its concrete, historical expressions in the mysteries of Christ. The Catholic Mass is an enactment of this mystagogical remembering. But the Catholic understanding of the Mass is that it is more than a memory. In the Mass, this love is more than a memory; it becomes a Presence.[35] In the Mass we both remember and encounter Christ. We say "Glory be!" And we say "Amen."

[35] "One's life is progressively being transformed" according to and in the celebration of God's sacrificial love, each and every Sunday. See Pope Benedict XVI, apostolic exhortation *Sacramentum caritatis* (February 22, 2007), no. 64c, http://www.vatican.va/content/benedict-xvi/en/apost_exhortations/documents/hf_ben-xvi_exh_20070222_sacramentum-caritatis.html.

We may thus extend our mystagogical reading of *The Magician's Nephew* to the whole liturgical year, from Advent, through Christmas, Lent, and Easter, to the feast of Christ the King, which anticipates his Second Coming. Each liturgical year brings us ever deeper into the mystery of Christ's love *for us*, to which the circling round conforms us each day, each week, and each year. This happens not only by encountering the mystery of Christ, but also the reality of Christ's "will of love" in the saints. The liturgical year remembers how the saints have exercised the dominion of God's love. The whole liturgical year therefore has a mystagogical element to it. Day by day, we see the unobservable, creative work of God become visible in the saints. The saints of the liturgical calendar are named and celebrated as models of heroic conformation to the mystery of God's love, whatever sacrifices this might ask of us. As the liturgical year leads us to celebrate the saints, it urges us to look into our own futures, and courageously imagine and hope that we too might become *saints* according to God's "dominion of love."[36]

---

[36] Pope Benedict XVI put it this way: "God made the world so that there could be a space where he might communicate his love, and from which the response of love might come back to him. From God's perspective, the heart of the man who responds to him is greater and more important than the whole immense material cosmos, for all that the latter allows us to glimpse something of God's grandeur." Pope Benedict XVI, Homily for the Easter Vigil, 2011.

VII

THE LAST BATTLE

On Knowing Him Here for a Little

Part VII

Madeline Infantine

To know him is to finally be
as happy as he means you to be.

To feel the heart leap (and now know why)
as dawn greets the end of dreams.

Here is the great bright procession,
mountain light, and the end
of all seeking.

Come, after the cold death of the sun,
to find warm daylight, flowers at foot,
blue sky above, and laughter in his eyes.

Land looked for, land longed for,
land loved and at last
                          known.

The Last Battle:
The End of the Beginning

Anthony Pagliarini

In the last days of Narnia, far up to the west beyond Lantern Waste and close beside the great waterfall, there lived an Ape. He was so old that no one could remember when he had first come to live in those parts, and he was the cleverest, ugliest, most wrinkled Ape you can imagine. He had a little house, built of wood and thatched with leaves, up in the fork of a great tree, and his name was Shift.

— *The Last Battle*, chap. 1

So begins the end of all things in Narnia. What culminates in the dramatic sounding of time's giant horn begins much earlier with the slow unraveling of what was given at the dawn of creation—both in our world and in that one. With an allusion to the story of Eden, Lewis begins *The Last Battle* by presenting us with the cleverest of creatures in the fork of a tree (cf. Gen 3). Narnia does not mean to be a simple parallel to this world of ours; there is no neat correspondence between one side of the wardrobe and the other. Even so, Lewis shows here in the Western Wilds of Narnia that very same rot that took hold in Eden. And I think that he couldn't truthfully do otherwise.

Shift, to be certain, is a peculiar kind of miscreant, but his sin is the foundational sin of all intellectual creatures, of any "Talking Beast"—namely, an abuse of words. Such a thing may not sound uniquely horrible—couldn't we name a host of more horrendous crimes?—but it is the distortion of language, and so of truth itself, that lays at the root of all destruction. And it is this abuse that Lewis has in mind to name as the cause of the world's end. He tells us as much with the names of his main characters, names that together suggest distortion of meaning and confusion: Shift and Puzzle.

Lewis' account of creation in *The Magician's Nephew* anticipates this end. As Digory, Polly, and the others look on, Aslan wakes the higher creatures of his new world. "Narnia. Narnia. Narnia, awake. Love. Think. Speak."[1] To the Talking Beasts the Lion entrusts the whole of what is made. "Creatures," says Aslan, "I give you yourselves.... I give you the woods, the fruits, the rivers. I give you the stars and I give you myself." Last of all, as both gift and responsibility, he hands on to them the care of the "Dumb Beasts." "Treat them gently," he warns, "and cherish them but do not go back to their ways lest you cease to be Talking Beasts. For out of them you were taken and into them you can return. Do not so."[2] Speech is the mark of exalted status, and it is the right use of speech in the work of tending and keeping the others that promises to preserve all that Aslan has given. The abuse of language, on the other hand, promises its undoing. Why?

For Saint Thomas Aquinas, judgment about reality— itself a kind of interior "word"—gives rise to an outer,

---

[1] *The Magician's Nephew*, 70, chap. 9.
[2] Ibid., 71, chap. 10.

spoken word which expresses that judgment.[3] This exter-
nalization is more than just a by-product of thought, more
than just a rippling out of something more essential already
complete in the mind. Rather, language is the means by
which we bring our freedom to bear on the world. When
I say "I love you" to my wife or children, I do more than
communicate a judgment of mine in an information-
giving sort of way. (If it were just that, there would be no
need to say it each day.) In speaking these words to them,
I bring that judgment to bear in such a way that we are
changed. Seen in this way, speech is the quintessential act
of a free creature.

Speech is also, fittingly, mankind's first act in the pages
of Scripture. We are the image of a God who speaks a
world into being and who asks us to speak so that we
might draw that world into right relation and into rest. No
matter that Adam, in that first moment of speaking, doesn't
find a helpmate among all the livestock, the birds in the
sky, and all the wild animals (Gen 2:20). By naming them,
he sets all things in right relation; he "orders all things
well" (Wis 8:1) and so exercises that dominion which is
nothing other than an extension of the divine work of
naming things into existence. We are talking beasts, and
our speech is not just a making audible of our intellect,
not just a transmission in some medium or other. Speech
is what renders truth in the service of love, is what allows
us to exercise our unique role of tending and keeping (cf.
Gen 1:26, 28; 2:8). The communion of this world, like
the Trinitarian communion it images, is begotten and preserved in speech, in the Word. And the failure of speech is
the paradigmatic failure of humanity, and, for that matter,
of all Talking Beasts.

[3] See *Summa Theologica* I, q. 34, art. 1.

The philosopher Joseph Pieper explains this nicely:

[Plato's] objection [to the Sophists] could be summed up
in these brief terms: corruption of the word—you are
corrupting the language! ... Word and language form the
medium that sustains the common existence of the human
spirit as such. The reality of the word in eminent ways
makes existential interaction happen. And so if the word
becomes corrupted, human existence itself will not remain
unaffected and untainted.... Human words and language
accomplish a twofold purpose.... Since the accomplish-
ment is twofold, we may already here suspect that the
word's degeneration and corruption can also be twofold.
First, words convey reality. We speak in order to name
and identify something that is real, to identify it for *someone*, of course—and this points to the second aspect in
question, the interpersonal character of human speech.[4]

Said again, the communion of this world, like the Trinitarian communion it images, is begotten and preserved in
the Word. And again, the failure of speech is the paradigmatic failure of humanity and, for that matter, of all Talking
Beasts. Isn't it the case that the breakdown of communion,
both in Eden and in the Western Wilds of Narnia, begins
with that cleverest of creatures in the fork of the tree and
his question "Did God really say ...?" (cf. Gen 3:1). In the
first, the breakdown begins by introducing suspicion about
the truthfulness of the Lord's words and so also the Lord's
own goodness and love. In Narnia, it begins with a similar
twisting—or shifting. We are made to wonder about the
content of Aslan's "speech" and about who it is that might
convey that content truthfully:

[4]Josef Pieper, *Abuse of Language—Abuse of Power*, trans. Lothar Kraus (San
Francisco: Ignatius Press, 1992), 14–15.

"Well then, that's settled," said the Ape. "You will pretend to be Aslan, and I'll tell you what to say."

"No, no, no," said Puzzle. "Don't say such dreadful things. It would be wrong, Shift. I may be not very clever but I know that much. What would become of us if the real Aslan turned up?"

"I expect he'd be very pleased," said Shift.[5]

Just then thunder boomed above their heads, making the earth shake beneath them and knocking both animals to the ground. As soon as Puzzle recovered his breath, he turned to Shift and said, "There! ... It's a sign, a warning. I knew we were doing something dreadfully wicked. Take this wretched skin off me at once." But Shift, whose mind, Lewis tells us, worked very quickly, immediately responded: "No, no.... It's a sign the other way. I was just going to say that if the real Aslan, as you call him, meant us to go on with this, he would send us a thunderclap and an earth-tremor.... You've got to do it now, Puzzle.... You know you don't understand these things. What could a donkey know about signs?"[6]

"It's a sign the other way," Shift says, and with that, things begin to go dreadfully "the other way." Here, with Shift, Lewis doesn't mean to give us an account of the moment of original sin. (We are told of that in *The Magician's Nephew* both when Digory rings the bell on Charn and when Jadis steals into the hidden garden at the dawn of Narnia.) What Lewis does mean, I think, is to unfold the end to which that sin leads, to the last battle it brings about and to indicate what, in the last instance, is the only antidote to that sin. *The Last Battle* is a dramatization of the

---

[5] *The Last Battle*, 674, chap. 1.
[6] Ibid.

breakdown of communion and, with it, the increasing difficulty of knowing the truth. It is, in other words, a book about the high cost of deceit and of the virtue of faith.

Knowledge and Love

In his discussion of Plato and the Sophists, Josef Pieper points to something puzzling about our use of human reason:

> [Hegel] called the sophists of Socrates' time "extremely refined and learned people"; but such praise, in Hegel's manner of speaking, sounds somewhat ambiguous. It is precisely such learned refinement, says Hegel, such absolute and unmoored questioning that plucks apart any object and dialectically discredits everything; it is such "refined reasoning" (*gebildetes Raisonnement*)—an expression repeatedly used by Hegel—that poses the true danger. It almost inevitably leads us, says Hegel, to the conviction that everything can be justified if we look hard enough for reasons. To quote Hegel: "You need not have advanced very far in your learning in order to find good reasons even for the most evil of things. All the evil deeds in this world since Adam and Eve have been justified with good reasons." Hegel, therefore, sees here a danger clearly intrinsic to the human mind being part of its nature, a danger that can perhaps be overcome but never entirely avoided.[7]

Shift is a fine and learned ape. In a way analogous to God in the opening pages of Scripture, his speech generates a world. His speech does not call anything into being—not really—but it does shape how it is that Puzzle and the

[7] Pieper, *Abuse of Language*, 8–9.

others are able to see reality. He is full of many "good reasons" about what has come to pass and what should. In a way that is coherent and persuasive, he renders an account of "the real" that is all but invincible. When, for instance, Tirian waits in the shadows on Stable Hill ready to show Puzzle to the crowds, Shift uses the fake Aslan's absence to his advantage.

> Now listen, all of you. A terrible thing has happened.... And Aslan ... is very angry about it.... At this very moment, when the Terrible One himself is among us— there in the stable just behind me—one wicked Beast has chosen to do what you'd think no one would dare to do even if He were a thousand miles away. It has dressed itself up in a lion-skin and is wandering about in these very woods pretending to be Aslan.... It's a Donkey! A common, miserable Ass![8]

Poggin is right to lament Shift's "cursed, cursed cleverness!" By mixing "a little truth" he makes his "lie far stronger."[9] Even so, Shift's lies are vulnerable. The Talking Beasts of Narnia love Aslan, and that very love shapes their understanding of what is fitting to do. Indeed, as Saint Gregory the Great teaches, "love itself is a kind of knowledge," and by this they already know what becomes the Lion.[10] What resistance the animals possess they possess not in virtue of being cleverer than Shift, but in virtue of having a greater love.

Puzzle's reaction to the discovery of the lion skin at Caldron Pool is a perfect (and touching) example of this virtue of love:

[8] *The Last Battle*, 723, chap. 9.

[9] Ibid.

[10] Gregory the Great, "Homily 27," in *Forty Gospel Homilies*, trans. Dom David Hurst (Kalamazoo, MI: Cistercian Publications, 1990), 215.

"I wonder who killed the poor lion," said Puzzle presently. "It ought to be buried. We must have a funeral."

"Oh, it wasn't a Talking Lion," said Shift.... "This skin must have belonged to a dumb, wild lion." ...

"All the same, Shift," said Puzzle, "even if the skin only belonged to a dumb, wild lion, oughtn't we to give it a decent burial? I mean, aren't all lions rather—well, rather solemn? Because of you know Who. Don't you see?... I don't think it would be respectful to the Great Lion, to Aslan himself, if an ass like me went about dressed up in a lion-skin," said Puzzle.[11]

The same is true of the Lamb, whose piety makes him more perceptive than Shift might wish. As one who knows the shepherd (cf. Jn 10:14), the Lamb objects to the ape's claim that Tash and Aslan are the same:

"Please," said the Lamb, "I can't understand. What have we to do with the Calormenes? We belong to Aslan. They belong to Tash. They have a god called Tash. They say he has four arms and the head of a vulture. They kill Men on his altar. I don't believe there's any such person as Tash. But if there was, how could Aslan be friends with him?"

All the animals cocked their heads sideways and all their bright eyes flashed toward the Ape. They knew it was the best question anyone had asked yet.[12]

We are not told what becomes of the Lamb, but a good many of the animals do remain with Shift. Having the right intuitions about Aslan is one thing. Knowing well what he will do is another. In *Prince Caspian*, Lucy meets Aslan and is distraught that he will not now so easily show himself to the others as once he did. "Oh dear, oh dear,"

---

[11] *The Last Battle*, 671–72, chap. 1.
[12] Ibid., 685, chap. 3.

says Lucy, "And I was so pleased at finding you again.... And I thought you'd come roaring in and frighten all the enemies away—like last time. And now everything is going to be horrid." "It is hard for you, little one," says Aslan. "But things never happen the same way twice."[13] As we are told so often in the chronicles, Aslan is not a tame lion. And so while the Lamb is right to question Shift's claims about Aslan and Tash—"How could Aslan be friends with him?"—knowing just what the Lion will do is not something we can see in advance. "He is," says Jewel in reply to Roonwit's reading of the heavens, "not a slave of the stars but their maker."[14]

The King and the Lord

The central question, then, of *The Last Battle* is this: Where is the voice of Aslan? Where is the sacrament of his presence whereby the good beasts of Narnia might know what to do?

Shift cleverly claims the mantle of prophecy for himself. Especially in moments when his story begins to wear thin, he makes appeal to his own authority. "I'm a man," he says. "If I look like an Ape, that's because I'm so very old.... And it's because I'm so old that I'm so wise. And it's because I'm so wise that I'm the only one Aslan is ever going to speak to.... He'll tell me what you've got to do, and I'll tell the rest of you."[15]

Unlike the sin in Eden, where Eve is made to distrust the Lord, the animals do not slack in their love for Aslan.

---

[13] *Prince Caspian*, 381, chap. 10.
[14] *The Last Battle*, 677, chap. 2.
[15] Ibid., 684, chap. 3.

As Puzzle before them, they go along with Shift's plan because they are made to believe, however haltingly, that Aslan has allowed Shift to speak in his name. "Why we— we wanted him to come back to Narnia," says one of the mice. And it is their love of the Lion that moves them to obedience, even if "he seems to have come back very angry this time."[16]

Things begin to turn, however, with the arrival of Tirian. While they resign themselves to the fact of "Aslan" speaking though Shift, the animals are not yet overcome. In their love of the king, they alight, unknowingly at first, upon the genuine site of Aslan's presence. Obedience to the king, whose office and very person recapitulate the whole history of Aslan's providence in Narnia, becomes the means by which the animals begin to understand Shift's lies for what they are. We see this most clearly in their visit to Tirian after he is captured by the Calormenes and bound to a tree.

> When it was almost dark Tirian heard a light pitter-patter of feet and saw some small creatures coming toward him....
>
> "Lord King! dear Lord King," said their shrill voices, "we are so sorry for you. We daren't untie you because Aslan might be angry with us. But we've brought you your supper."
>
> ...
>
> "Little friends," said Tirian, "how can I thank you for all this?"
>
> "You needn't, you needn't," said the little voices. "What else could we do? *We don't want any other King.* We're your people. If it was only the Ape and the Calormenes who were against you we would have fought till

[16] Ibid., 689, chap. 4.

we were cut into pieces before we'd have let them tie you up. We would, we would indeed. But we can't go against Aslan."

"Do you think it really is Aslan," said the King....

"There's no doubt about it. Everyone says it is Aslan's orders. And we've seen him." ...

"I suppose what we're doing now may be wrong," said the Rabbit.

"I don't care if it is," said one of the Moles. "I'd do it again."[17]

On the one hand, the animals believe they should be faithful to "Aslan's" commands. They don't wish to upset him. Though he has been terrible to them, they try even to judge charitably all that he does. "We must all have done something dreadfully wrong without knowing it,"[18] says the mouse. All the same, they will not slack in their devotion to Tirian, whom they address, rightly, as "Lord King! dear Lord King!"

What I think Lewis wishes us to see here is that the devotion to Aslan and the devotion to Tirian are one and the same. The Lion and the one who reigns under the standard of the Red Lion of Narnia can't be set in opposition. The rabbits and the moles and the mice know this, and though they can't work out how, in the present, the one is to square with the other, they do not fail in their faithfulness to Tirian. There is, after all, only one King, and "we don't want any other king."[19] Just as there is only one England and one Narnia—though there be, as we see at the book's end, England and the England within, and Narnia and the Narnia within. One is the image of the

[17] Ibid., 687–89, chap. 4.
[18] Ibid., 689, chap. 4.
[19] Ibid., 688, chap. 4.

other. Or to frame it more positively, one is the sacrament of the other. So too there is only one King, and to
honor "Lord King! dear Lord King [Tirian]!" is to honor
the Great King, the Lion (and so too the Emperor-over-
the-Sea). What the beasts instinctively understand is that
Tirian is the sacrament of the Lion's presence. Aslan is
not so absent as Shift would have them believe in saying
to Puzzle that "he never *does* turn up, you know. Not
nowadays."[20]

What does it mean to say that Tirian is the presence of
Aslan? As we'll come to see, Tirian himself struggles to
understand just who Aslan is and how he will act. Here
the question of sacramentality merges with what was said
above about the role and function of language. The communion of this world, like the Trinitarian communion it
images, is begotten and preserved in speech, in the Word.
Those who speak truthfully are themselves sacraments of
the Word, who is himself the font and origin of every
word, as Saint Thomas says.[21] Truthful speech creates. It
preserves and strengthens that communion—that "very
good" (Gen 1:26)—which God created in the beginning
and which he restored in the Incarnation by the full speaking of his Word into the human condition. If Tirian, as
I've just suggested, is the sacrament of Aslan's presence, he
is so because in his words and his very flesh he is the living repository of the Word. Tirian embodies all that God
reveals and is himself the "place" where Aslan might be
met. In this way, Tirian is an image of the Church—the
"Body of Christ" (see 1 Cor 1:12–27)—whose life (including her acts of repentance) preserves in all of its integrity
what God has revealed in his coming among us. She is

[20] Ibid., 674, chap. 1.
[21] Cf. Thomas Aquinas, *Super ad Hebraeos*, no. 217.

"the sacrament of salvation."[22] So also Tirian, in whom the good beasts of Narnia encounter the Great Lion.

With this in mind, we should notice how Lewis presents Tirian's suffering as an image of Christ's Passion. He is beat by the guards and then, with the crowds in a frenzy, Shift shouts, "Take him away! Take him away ... and tie him to a tree."[23] It's not long before he is given wine to drink from "a little wooden cup ... being held to his lips."[24] And then there is the anguished cry of his prayer "Aslan, Aslan, come and help us now.... Let *me* be killed. I ask nothing for myself. But come and save all Narnia."[25] We might say, with the author of Hebrews, that "in the days of his flesh, Jesus offered up prayers and supplications, with loud cries and tears, to him who was able to save him from death, and he was heard for his godly fear. Although he was a Son, he learned obedience through what he suffered" (Heb 5:7-8).

Tirian is a Christ figure—someone who lays down his life for his friends (cf. Jn 15:13). And as such, Lewis wishes us to see Tirian as the antithesis of Shift, as the one whose disinterested truthfulness is the antidote to Shift's deception. Tirian really is the site of communion and is thus an image of the Church. What is so remarkable, and so oddly comforting, is that Tirian's camp, and Tirian himself, is full of uncertainty. To speak of Tirian as some kind of bastion of truthfulness doesn't, in the first instance, mean that he has everything worked out in full. (Nor does it

[22] Vatican Council II, Dogmatic Constitution on the Church *Lumen gentium* (November 21, 1964), no. 48, https://www.vatican.va/archive/hist_councils /ii_vatican_council/documents/vat-ii_const_19641121_lumen-gentium _en.html.

[23] *The Last Battle*, 686, chap. 3.

[24] Ibid., 688, chap. 4.

[25] Ibid., 690-91, chap. 4.

mean that he himself is upright in all his actions. Like the Church, his holiness is perhaps best seen in his repentance.) It means, rather, that Tirian—even when he has nothing to gain, even when there is no external force compelling him to do so, even when it concerns his own failings, even when it involves the risk of death—seeks to know Aslan and all things in light of Aslan. This is wonderfully clear in the conversation between him and Jewel after they've ambushed and killed two Calormenes whom they found whipping a Narnian horse. Tirian is overcome with the ignobility of their deed, and Jewel is likewise filled with shame. The horse's claim that his own beating was by Aslan's orders mixes in confusion with Tirian and Jewel's sorrow. Jewel cannot comprehend how Aslan could command such dreadful things, to which Tirian responds: "How should we know what he would do? We, who are murderers. Jewel, I will go back. I will give up my sword and put myself in the hands of these Calormenes and ask that they bring me before Aslan. Let him do justice on me."[26] Jewel knows this will mean that the Calormenes will kill Tirian as they claim the authority of Aslan, but Tirian is undeterred:

> "Do you think I care if Aslan dooms me to death?" said the King. "That would be nothing, nothing at all. Would it not be better to be dead than to have this horrible fear that Aslan has come and is not like the Aslan we have believed in and longed for? It is as if the sun rose one day and were a black sun."
>
> "I know," said Jewel. "Or as if you drank water and it were dry water. You are in the right, Sire. This is the end of all things. Let us go and give ourselves up."[27]

[26] Ibid., 682, chap. 3.
[27] Ibid.

In the course of the narrative, it is this decision—this resolute desire to seek Aslan's face—that brings Tirian (and Jewel) to Stable Hill at the very moment when Shift's lie is at its worst, when he gets around to saying: "Tash is only another name for Aslan. All that old idea of us being right and the Calormenes wrong is silly. We know better now. The Calormenes use different words but we all mean the same thing. Tash and Aslan are only two different names for you know Who. That's why there can never be any quarrel between them. Get that into your heads, you stupid brutes. Tash is Aslan: Aslan is Tash."[28]

Tirian, like the little lamb who speaks before him, knows at least that this is a lie and confronts Shift: "Ape," he cries with a great voice, "you lie damnably. You lie like a Calormene. You lie like an Ape."[29] And it is this that sets Tirian's Passion in motion and begins the whole process of sifting that comes to a head in the last battle.

Emeth and the Dwarfs

Tirian's actions bring about a final victory, or at least a portion of one. The possibility of real loss remains and will in fact be, in Lewis' telling, a feature of the end. At the close of Narnia, not everyone passes through the doorway into Aslan's country. Some of the Talking Beasts, at the sight of Aslan, are filled with "fear and hatred," though only for a moment. Like Ginger the cat, they cease to be Talking Beasts. They are *un*created and then they disappear "into his huge black shadow, which ... streamed away to the left of the doorway."[30]

[28] Ibid., 685, chap. 3.
[29] Ibid., 686, chap. 3.
[30] Ibid., 751, chap. 14.

As we have seen, Aslan's presence is a mediated presence. Membership in a real flesh-and-blood communion—the kingdom of Narnia under the leadership of Tirian—is both the means and the site of one's communion with Aslan. To lose faith in the very possibility of human communion, to view all things with suspicion, severs one from fellowship with God and plunges him into a permanent isolation. The real horror of Shift's deception is not the felling of Lantern Waste or the impending takeover of Narnia by the Calormenes, but its giving rise to a suspicion that all communion is orchestrated by self-interest and all speech by a will to power.

So it is with the Dwarfs. When we first meet them in *The Last Battle*, the Dwarfs are under the charge of two Calormenes. "Has the Tisroc fought a great battle, Dwarfs, and conquered your land," Tirian asks, "that thus you go patiently to die in the salt-pits of Pugrahan?" "Aslan's orders, Aslan's orders," they reply, "He's sold us. What can we do against *him?*"[31] These good creatures believe in Aslan. They are rightly sore at what they believe he's done to them, but they believe in him. Tirian draws Puzzle into view and proves that "it has all been a lie. Aslan has not come to Narnia at all. You have been cheated by the Ape." They join in the fight and kill the Calormenes, but then, when "there was no enemy left," the Dwarfs do not respond with a renewed love for the real Aslan but with unbelief:

> "Now, Dwarfs, you are free. Tomorrow I will lead you to free all Narnia. Three cheers for Aslan!"
>
>   . . .
>
> "Well," said the Black Dwarf (whose name was Griffle), "I don't know how all you chaps feel, but I feel I've

[31] Ibid., 705, chap. 7.

heard as much about Aslan as I want to for the rest of my life."

"That's right, that's right," growled the other Dwarfs. "It's all a plant, all a blooming plant."

. . .

"Do you mean you don't believe in the real Aslan?" said Jill. "But I've seen him. And he has sent us two here out of a different world."

"Ah," said Griffle with a broad smile. "So *you* say . . ."

"Churl," cried Tirian, "will you give a lady the lie to her very face?"

"You keep a civil tongue in your head, Mister," replied the Dwarf. "I don't think we want any more Kings—if you *are* Tirian, which you don't look like him—no more than we want any Aslans. . . ."

"That's right," said the other Dwarfs. "We're on our own now. No more Aslan, no more Kings, no more silly stories about other worlds. The Dwarfs are for the Dwarfs."[32]

The Dwarfs have come to suspect everything. They are hardened for having been fooled. Not unreasonably, they close themselves to any encounter with the real Lion. And so, when in the end they pass through the doorway into Aslan's country, they are incapable of knowing just where it is they are. They are like Uncle Andrew at the dawn of Narnia, about whom Aslan says, "He has made himself unable to hear my voice. If I spoke to him, he would hear only growlings and roarings. Oh Adam's sons, how cleverly you defend yourselves against all that might do you good!"[33] So too the Dwarfs: "You see," says Aslan. "They will not let us help them. They have chosen cunning instead of belief. Their prison is only in their own

[32] Ibid., 706–7, chap. 7.
[33] Lewis, *The Magician's Nephew*, 98, chap. 14.

minds, yet they are in that prison; and so afraid of being
taken in that they cannot be taken out."[34]

There is the possibility of real loss. The Dwarfs are in
large measure victims of the crowd long since carried off
by Tash, but there is no easy way, or perhaps any way,
of healing what they've become. "Dearest," says Aslan to
Lucy about Dwarfs, "I will show you both what I can, and
what I cannot, do."[35]

In contrast with the Dwarfs, whose fate is itself cor-
porate and is in large measure set by the wider human
(dis)communion, the righteous Calormene Emeth stands
in isolation. He worships what is unmistakably a demon,
and if we take the Lamb at his word, Emeth is likely to have
been part of the human blood offered on the altar of Tash.
And yet he is welcome in Aslan's country. Why? Although,
in one respect, he believes wrongly, Emeth is, like Tirian,
one who is truthful. In the passage below, notice how time
and again he gives Aslan, whom he now knows as the Lord,
every reason why he, Emeth, should not be accepted. His
words, like those of Tirian after the murder, are not self-
interested in the least. Emeth—the one whose name in
Hebrew means "truth"—desires the truth and speaks truly.
In this way, he has all the while been longing for Aslan, and
so receives him as a reward. Though he knew nothing of
that flesh-and-blood communion centered in Narnia, his
longing for the truth allows him to find "him whom [his]
soul loves" (Song 3:4). "For," as Aslan says, "all find what
they truly seek."[36] Emeth tells of his encounter with Aslan
in this way:

> The Glorious One bent down his golden head and
> touched my forehead with his tongue and said, Son, thou

[34] *The Last Battle*, 748, chap. 13.
[35] Ibid., 747, chap. 13.
[36] Ibid., 757, chap. 15.

art welcome. But I said, Alas, Lord, I am no son of thine
but the servant of Tash. He answered, Child, all the service thou hast done to Tash, I account as service done to
me.... If any man swear by Tash and keep his oath for the
oath's sake, it is by me that he has truly sworn, though he
know it not, and it is I who reward him. And if any man
do a cruelty in my name, then, though he says the name
Aslan, it is Tash whom he serves and by Tash his deed is
accepted. Dost thou understand, Child? I said, Lord, thou
knowest how much I understand.[37]

And in truth, it may well be that Emeth was not really
much farther off than Tirian and all of Narnia. For every
similarity between what was known below and what is
known above, there is an ever greater dissimilarity. All
are newcomers to Aslan's country. The Narnia within—
however much it be the same place as the Narnia we have
known—is nevertheless more unlike it than not. As Jewel
says when looking at the real Narnia in Aslan's country: "I
have come home at last! This is my real country! I belong
here. This is the land I have been looking for all my life,
though I never knew it till now. The reason why we loved
the old Narnia is that it sometimes looked a little like this.
Bree-hee-hee! Come further up, come further in!"[38]

The End

"We speak," Pieper said, "in order to name and identify something that is real, to identify it for *someone*, of
course."[39] The gift of speech—the grace of being a
Talking Beast—is that we might render the truth in the

[37] Ibid., 756–57, chap. 15.
[38] Ibid., 760, chap. 15.
[39] Pieper, *Abuse of Language*, 15.

service of love. There is, in Lewis' vision, only an analogy between this world and the real world of Aslan's country, but if we would know that country at all, it requires that we speak truthfully even here and, in the likeness of Tirian or Emeth, that we become vulnerable to the word of another, the word of one who is "not a tame Lion" and who speaks freely in and through those who bear his standard. It means, in other words, entering into the human communion "here below," for the story that takes place "further up and further in" is not a new story, but a drawing in of all that is already begun here below.

For all of its emphasis on the hereafter and the incommensurable delight and beauty of Aslan's country, we should be keen to notice that the greatest joy in that land is one which already took root and was enjoyed in this one, in the real flesh-and-blood communion of this time and this place, among all those who, like Roonwit, "drink first to Aslan and truth, Sire, and secondly to your Majesty."[40]

[40] The Last Battle, 676, chap. 2.

CONTRIBUTORS

Stephen Barany, MFA, M.Div., is an illustrator from South Bend, Indiana, specializing in ink. His illustrations often provide multiple levels of engagement by combining small, symbolic drawings into larger, thoughtfully composed arrays.

Catherine Rose Cavadini, Ph.D., is Associate Teaching Professor at the University of Notre Dame, where she also directs the Master of Arts Program in Theology. She teaches courses on the saints, scriptural interpretation, and Church history.

Leonard J. DeLorenzo, Ph.D., is Associate Professor of the Practice in the McGrath Institute for Church Life and teaches theology at the University of Notre Dame. He is the author or editor of several books, including *Work of Love: A Theological Reconstruction of the Communion of Saints*; *Turn to the Lord: Forming Disciples for Lifelong Conversion*; and *Dante, Mercy, and the Beauty of the Human Person* (editor).

David W. Fagerberg, Ph.D., is Professor of Theology at the University of Notre Dame. His publications include *On Liturgical Theology*, *Liturgical Mysticism*, and *Liturgical Dogmatics*.

Madeline Infantine, MFA, MTS, is a poet and writer who also serves as an academic advisor for first-year students at the University of Notre Dame. Her work has appeared in *Notre Dame Magazine, Church Life Journal*, and *Presence: A Journal of Catholic Poetry*, among other publications.

Rebekah Lamb, Ph.D., is a Lecturer (Assistant Professor) in Theology and the Arts at the School of Divinity in the University of Saint Andrews. She principally teaches within the school's Institute of Theology, Imagination, and the Arts (ITIA). She specializes in religion and literature from the long nineteenth century to the present and has published in *The Journal of Pre-Raphaelite Studies, Religions, Church Life Journal, New Blackfriars, Theology in Scotland*, and elsewhere. She is writing a book on boredom and aesthetics in the Victorian period and late modernity with McGill-Queen's University Press.

Francesca Aran Murphy, Ph.D., is Professor of Theology at the University of Notre Dame. Her publications include *God Is Not a Story, Art and Intellect in the Philosophy of Étienne Gilson, Christ the Form of Beauty*, and *Gnosis and the Theocrats from Mars*.

Anthony J. Pagliarini, Ph.D., is Assistant Teaching Professor in the Department of Theology at the University of Notre Dame. He specializes in the Old Testament and is currently authoring a commentary on Jeremiah. As the Director of Undergraduate Studies in Theology, he teaches and advises the department's over five hundred majors and minors.

Peter J. Schakel, Ph.D., is Peter C. and Emajean Cook Professor of English Emeritus at Hope College in Holland, Michigan. An internationally respected student of C. S. Lewis' work, he has written or edited seven books about

Lewis, including *Imagination and the Arts in C. S. Lewis* and *The Way into Narnia: A Reader's Guide*.

Father Michael Ward, Ph.D., is Senior Research Fellow at Blackfriars Hall, University of Oxford, and Professor of Apologetics at Houston Baptist University, Texas. His publications include *Planet Narnia: The Seven Heavens in the Imagination of C. S. Lewis*, *The Cambridge Companion to C. S. Lewis* (editor), and *After Humanity: A Guide to C. S. Lewis' The Abolition of Man*.

BIBLIOGRAPHICAL NOTE

All citations to the Chronicles of Narnia series derive from the 2001 single-volume edition by HarperCollins.

All quoted text from the Narnia series is copyrighted by C. S. Lewis Pte. Ltd., as outlined on page 4 of this volume.